THE PAN BOOK
OF SAILING

THE PAN BOOK OF
SAILING

Group-Captain
F. H. L. SEARL
Chief Instructor, Emsworth Sailing School

A PAN ORIGINAL

Revised Edition 1967

PAN BOOKS LTD : LONDON

First published 1964 by
PAN BOOKS LTD
33 Tothill Street, London, S.W.1

2nd Printing (revised) 1967

PRINTED AND BOUND IN ENGLAND BY
HAZELL WATSON AND VINEY LTD
AYLESBURY, BUCKS

CONTENTS

ILLUSTRATIONS
IN PHOTOGRAVURE

between pages 88 and 89

The LEADER, a multi-purpose sailing dinghy of high performance which is suitable for the newcomer

The WAYFARER, a sturdy 16-ft high-performance dinghy which also makes a good family boat

The ZENITH, crew watching warily as the spinnaker pulls them downwind

The TRICORN, a popular first boat which combines the sailing qualities of a class dinghy with two-berth accommodation
(Photo: Beken, Cowes)

The ALBACORE, a 15-ft racing dinghy which is also a very suitable family boat

The MIRROR dinghy, which has grown very rapidly in numbers over a short period

The SHEARWATER catamaran, one of the most successful multi-hull designs

The *Yachting World* CADET, a classic racing dinghy for juniors up to sixteen years of age
(Photo: Courtesy of Group Captain E. F. Haylock)

between pages 136 and 137

The NATIONAL ENTERPRISE, being raced here in Poole Harbour by the designer Jack Holt and his wife

The JOLLYBOAT, a very fast dinghy here being ballasted to windward by the trapeze
(Photo: Beken, Cowes)

The *Yachting World* SOLO, a popular dinghy being sailed here by Jack Holt the designer
(Photo: Courtesy of *Yachting World*)

The Fairey FIREFLY, a high-performance racing dinghy here seen planing on a broad reach

(Photo: Courtesy of Eileen Ramsay)

Four *Sunday Times* SIGNETs, seen leaving St Margaret's Bay for Calais which was reached $4\frac{1}{2}$ hours later

(Photo: Courtesy of Thomson Newspapers Ltd.)

Dambuster, a beautiful ocean-racing yacht

(Photo: Beken, Cowes)

Maica, a French-owned ocean-racing yacht

(Photo: Beken, Cowes)

The Fairey FISHERMAN, a power boat which follows some traditional lines based on offshore fishing craft

(Photo: Beken, Cowes)

The Dell Quay RANGER, a 25-ft four-berth high-speed luxury cruiser

(Photo: Courtesy of Dell Quay Sales Ltd.
'White Unicorn' loaned for the purpose by H. Godfrey, Esq.)

FOREWORD

By Lt.-General Sir Brian Horrocks,
K.C.B., K.B.E., D.S.O.,
M.C., LL.D (Hon).

In the past 'Yachting' was very much the perquisite of the Aristocracy, who were the only people with enough time and money to enjoy this expensive sport. Now, thank goodness, all this has changed – small boats are comparatively inexpensive and more people from every walk of life are finding themselves with increased leisure at their disposal. In fact, many are beginning to wonder what to do with their spare time.

Any man who leads a well-filled life must have a private lane down which to escape to another world – preferably as remote as possible in feeling and tempo from his everyday existence.

For some the lane leads to a garden, or shelves of books, or a workshop in which absorbed hours can be spent with wood, tools, glue, nails and screws. The essential thing, I think, is that the lane should lead away from ever-ringing telephones, radio, television, pavements filled with hurrying, elbowing crowds, and roads congested with impatient, hastening drivers.

For the past seven years my lane has led down to a quiet water's edge where a boat lies at her moorings. At the age of sixty-one I attended, with my wife, a course in small-boat sailing, first of all at Bosham and then at Emsworth Sailing School. Now we have found something which occupies all our spare time most happily – I only wish that I had taken it up many years ago.

So you see, it is never too late to start and I commend this particular lane to everyone – old and young alike.

Once you are aboard and your craft heads out into the harbour, all the irritations and frustrations of modern life seem to melt away. The only things that matter are the pulse of the restless sea, felt through the tiller, and the chuckle and talk of the water against the side of the boat.

If you wish to penetrate this particular lane for yourself, or want an interesting book of reference, I strongly recommend this *Pan Book of Sailing*, which as far as I can see contains everything that anyone could possibly want to know.

The author – Group Captain F. H. L. Searl – known to his friends as 'Crab' – not on account of any particular aquatic activities, but because on one notable occasion he apparently flew an aircraft sideways – has figured prominently in my nautical education, first as an Instructor at Bosham, and then in charge of his own Sailing School at Emsworth. He is one of those fortunate men who are able to combine business with pleasure because he loves the sea and all to do with it. Over the years he has acquired a vast store of knowledge about sailing and all its different aspects.

As I write this foreword in my small cottage at Emsworth, I can see from my window – looking over Chichester Harbour – a dozen or so cheerful figures in yellow oilskins setting off in 'Wayfarer' sailing dinghies belonging to his Emsworth Sailing School. In the evening, tired but happy, they will return to port more determined than ever that their particular escape lane will eventually lead to a boat, whether it sails on river, lake or – best of all – on the sea.

BRIAN G. HORROCKS

PREFACE

FOR some years past my work has been to teach people of all ages to sail, usually from scratch. Later on I have had to advise my pupils what sort of boat to buy, for first things must come first. About two-thirds of my pupils are over forty and most of them come from medicine, law, accountancy and the kind of job which means worrying for most of the working day. All of them want to get out in a boat, somehow.

No doubt this springs from the theory that if you scratch an inhabitant of these islands you find either a sailor or a farmer. Much of the common coin of our everyday speech derives from the sea. 'Sailing too close to the wind', 'not liking the cut of his jib', 'by and large' and even 'taking the gilt off the gingerbread' came into common use through sailors. Instinct in our blood is the feeling for the sea shared by all islanders and today this is coupled with a need to get off the roads, to be free of the bondage of the internal combustion engine, and just to get away from it all. Escapism, if you like, but what is wrong with escapism?

No experience will ever quite equal that of sailing a boat entirely by yourself for the first time, unless it be that of your first sail in the first boat you own.

Enjoy your pipe dreams, however much modified they may be by growing experience, and if that cruise to Cherbourg ends up by being a potter round the Solent ports what of it? You will make Cherbourg next year. Or the year after.

Since the war every suitable creek, river, lake and gravel pit blossoms with sails from early spring until late autumn. I address my book to all of you who have so far only stood and watched.

*Dedicated to the pupil who came and
stayed on: we lived happily ever after*

CHAPTER 1

GETTING STARTED

Choosing a Base – Where to Learn – What to Wear

ONCE I heard a man say: 'They'll always cross the road to look at a boat.'

This is so true. Tow a boat on a trailer, sail into a creek by a car park and there are at once a dozen watching with curiosity. There is something compelling in the matter of leaving dry land. It has the spice of excitement, the tang of new and unlearned skills. Even the everyday chores of taking care of a boat, the fitting of new gadgets, the wearisome scraping down, painting and varnishing have a beckoning appeal.

What I am really trying to avoid repeating is that over-quoted remark made by the Water Rat. There really is something in just messing about with a boat and for some of us it becomes a way of life. Times by the clock cease to matter very much and the ebb and flow of the tides set our timetable. Doctors might call it occupational therapy, for to handle a small boat successfully you can have no time to think of anything else.

One of my ex-pupils is a Member of Parliament obliged to listen, one hopes for the common good, to dreary debates on all kinds of dull subjects. He takes among his papers a tidetable and works out his weekend sailing programme. No doubt when he resumes his place on Monday his thoughts are mellowed by the recollection of the weekend.

The word 'yachting' has an expensive sound against a background of snobbery and privilege; in fact nothing could be more untrue, for there is a spirit of freemasonry afloat which is seldom met on land. From my own much-loved creek sail all kinds of people in all marches of life, and many do so on a shoestring budget. In a small boat they are all equal and only the good sailor is more equal than the others.

So I shall try to avoid the use of the word 'yachting'. It has a prohibitively expensive sound. It conjures pictures of luxury and it is not the takeover millionaires who will read this book. The majority take to the water in small boats and get more fun out of it than the owners of the really big yachts. My friend, Captain J. H. Illingworth, perhaps our greatest ocean-racing helmsman, is quite categorical about it: start in a sailing dinghy, for the principles are the same whatever the size. Bus Mosbacher, the America's Cup helmsman, crewed *Weatherly* with ex-small-boat sailors because as he says: 'racing a 12-metre is the same, only more so.'

The daily press refers to anything that floats as a 'yacht' without regard to its size. For me a yacht is something you can sleep in, spread yourself around in. We shall deal with boats up to 5 tons displacement and although this can be quite sizeable it barely qualifies. For one reason or another it may be that you will have to start in a larger boat. Don't buy anything larger than 5 tons and preferably something much smaller as your first boat. Leave buying a boat until you have learned something.

Mainly we shall be dealing with sailing craft but many are attracted to the small power boat. My own inclinations drive me away from the internal combustion engine. So much of everyday life hinges on the use of it that an escape is certainly a good thing. The guerilla war between sail and power is needless. There is selfishness on both sides in place of live and let live. None of this need exist if each side knew something of the other's problems, which often start with the new and inexperienced owner of a small power boat believing that because he can drive the family saloon he can handle his new pride and joy in a tideway.

Boats and women can be exasperating. Unlike women boats only do what the helmsman and conditions make them do. They are not possessed of some devil which makes them do unexpected things.

Good design helps them to help you. So long as you do not

ask your boat to do the impossible it will back you up.

The old order of yachting was an expensive one. Modern materials and design bring ownership within easy reach and a well-maintained boat will hold its value for many years. It may even appreciate as time goes on. Buying a car leaves the owner with an immediate depreciation in value before he has even left the showroom and the comparison is not a fair one. If you have the skill to build a boat yourself, you may do so for well under £100. The annual cost of your sailing if you live reasonably near some water can be less than that of playing golf or tennis.

It is not impossible to learn to handle a boat entirely by reading about the subject, just as it was once possible to learn to drive a car from a book. That was in the days before the roads were jammed with traffic and now there are too many craft afloat to allow of trial and error teach-yourself methods. Experience shows that skilled tuition combined with background reading brings the quickest and cheapest results.

It is logical to start by learning something about sailing before buying a boat, since nobody would dream of buying a car without having sat in one, let alone having learned to drive. Yet, carried away by some gleaming vision on a stand or in a showroom – and remember that all boats look so much bigger on land than they do in the water – people are every day buying sailing boats without ever having set foot in one.

It can be fatal to ask your knowledgeable friend what to buy, for he may not be as experienced as he appears to be. It is the nature of the small boat sailor to be wildly enthusiastic about the type of boat which he owns and this is just as it should be. But you may very quickly find yourself the owner of a terrifying racing machine when all you want to do is to potter about, for it all seems so easy when your friend takes you out for a sail. Do get some experience before you even think of buying a boat.

Sailing is all too often wistfully pictured as a pursuit for the young and nothing could be farther from the truth. I know one very good helmsman who started at sixty-one and now, at sixty-seven, his increasing skill and enthusiasm go along together. Another, who started at seventy-two, owns and sails a 16-ft dinghy with dash and enjoyment. Physical handicaps sometimes appear formidable but one of last year's pupils managed very well with a false leg and only the half of one hand. One of the *Sceptre* crew has two false legs, a leading dinghy helmsman was born without any legs at all, and beginners handicapped by the after-effects of polio come along every year.

Of course it is useful to be a good swimmer but, if you are not, one of the many excellent non-bulky lifejackets will take care of any emergency. Incidentally, the very last thing one does is to swim away from a capsized boat. Try to do it without a lifejacket and it may very well be the last thing that you do.

Choosing a Base

There is little point in learning to sail if you are not going on with it. Usually the ultimate aim is to own a boat, but if the exchequer will not run to this, crewing with an owner must substitute. You must consider where you are going to do your sailing when you have learned, and your choice of area is wide.

The rivers Thames, Severn, Trent and Dee come to mind at once. Then there are the Lakes, the Lochs of Scotland and, of course, the Norfolk Broads. Added to these are hundreds of lakes, reservoirs and gravel pits scattered all over Britain, although many of these latter may be reserved for the sole use of clubs which have leased them from the owners. A useful guide is *Getting Afloat* (3s. 6d. from Caravan Publications Ltd., 24 Store Street, London, W.C.1), which lists nearly 500 places where small boats may be launched or moored, what club facilities there are and a mass of information relevant to inland and tidal waters.

Many newcomers to sailing hold the belief that the first step is to join a club and be taught by it, but, with a very few exceptions, this is a vain hope. Most club members will have spent the dark winter thinking about getting out in a boat again and it is very understandable that they will not want to spend precious sailing time in teaching. Good helmsmen are not necessarily good teachers and many a beginner has been put off by being blinded by science at the outset. A very large number of clubs have had to refuse new and inexperienced candidates, so full are their lists, but it is usually a different matter when you can sail.

You will probably aim to join a sailing club eventually and most of them sponsor a class or classes. The sponsored class will be one best suited to the locality and you may even find that ownership, actual or projected, is a passport to membership. In many clubs the accent is very much on racing and the happy potterer may be a pariah. It is as well to spy out the land; if you spend your working week accumulating ulcers by worrying you may not feel like continuing the process over the weekend. There can be a lot of 'needle' in racing.

Any coastline is not necessarily suitable for a novice, for some are difficult and hazardous. It may well pay you to visit the area you have in mind.

Talk to a few local people, drop into the sailing club and get some advice, for sailing folk are always friendly and helpful. For many reasons the Solent and the great enclosed expanses of Chichester and Poole harbours provide an area in which to get started under the best conditions, but this does not rule out the Norfolk Broads, the rivers and the lakes. Unfortunately these latter areas are not well provided with teaching facilities.

Where to Learn

The national authority which fosters and encourages sailing is the Royal Yachting Association (171 Victoria Street, London, S.W.1 – Tate Gallery 4197). The Association keeps a register of teaching bodies, clubs and schools which it has approved and issues Certificates of Attendance. Possession of one of these Certificates is not yet obligatory but may very well be so in the near future. Already insurers are quoting less favourable rates to unqualified helmsmen. An appendix shows the syllabus laid down by the Royal Yachting Association, the form of Certificate and a list of those qualified to recommend its issue.

A letter to the Central Council of Physical Recreation (6 Bedford Square, London, W.C. 1) or to the Scottish Council for Physical Recreation (4 Queensferry Street, Edinburgh, 1) will bring you details of the facilities provided by these admirable bodies. State-aided, good and cheap courses are run at various centres on both inland and tidal waters. The only criticism one could have is that sometimes the quota of pupils to each instructor seems rather too high for sorting out the personal idiosyncrasies of each learner.

Any sailing course taken should be over a number of consecutive days if this is possible. However you set about it do get some skilled tuition. Sailing husbands should never try to teach their wives, for that way lies the Divorce Court!

What to Wear

You will need some clothes to sail in. This need not be an expensive matter.

Somebody once described the British Isles as having no climate – just weather. We have all learned to hope for the best whilst expecting the worst and nowhere can you get wetter and colder than afloat. If you are miserably uncomfortable you will learn very little. So it is very important to wear clothes which will keep you warm and dry.

You will probably start in a sailing dinghy and if this is in tidal waters you will almost certainly have to wade when launching the boat. So I shall start with the feet and work upwards.

Gum boots are out because in the case of a capsize they can fill with water and sink you even with a lifejacket. The ankle length type is acceptable but remember that a false step can fill them with water. If you are able to step aboard dry shod, canvas shoes with non-slip soles are excellent. Rope soles are not popular with some owners because they can pick up sand and grit which ruins varnish and paintwork.

My own preference is for the open mesh plastic sandals which most chandlers stock. Water quickly runs out and the feet are much warmer than in sodden canvas shoes and socks. If you feel that you cannot endure wet feet you can buy knee length synthetic rubber socks of the type worn by frogmen. These and trousers of the same material for winter sailing give a totally false impression of great toughness when wading out.

Jeans or old flannel trousers are a good foundation worn with a flannel shirt over a string vest. Top this with a thick woollen jersey of the greasy wool type – two, if you like. Remember that you can always shed clothes if it does turn out to be as hot as the weathermen predicted. There are very few days when shorts are bearable except on inland waters.

Next comes your personal buoyancy. If this is a waistcoat of the Marksway or Seaflote type it can be worn under the oil-skin smock or one piece suit which is your outer wear. Should you decide upon an inflatable or other more bulky lifejacket it will naturally have to be worn outside the oilskin. The Marksway or Seaflote type is preferable because it is not bulky and is always ready for use.

The outer layer is something really waterproof. Try it if you like but the old plastic raincoat you bought on the day when you were caught in the thunderstorm simply won't do when it comes to dealing with sheets of spray. A ski-ing anorak may serve in all except heavy weather, but you will be better off in something designed for the job. Most sailing schools hire out oilskins and lifejackets.

Something of a struggle to get in and out of, my own preference is for a one-piece oilskin suit having two sets of zip-fasteners down the front, two zip-fastened pockets and a belt. This is completely waterproof and I find myself wearing it for nine out of every ten sailing days in tidal waters between March and October. The alternative is oilskin trousers and smock – but see to it that the smock is really long enough to close the gap between the two garments.

In trying on oilskins remember that you may well be wearing two sweaters and a lifejacket underneath. Freedom of movement is essential and the material is one which will not stretch. Choose something on the large side rather than the small and if the trousers for this reason seem too long they can be shortened by a press stud arrangement sewn into some types, or they can be rolled up.

It is worth while to pay a little more for the better quality oilskins. Paper-thin types can be bought very cheaply and they usually last about ten minutes before tearing. If you can buy your goods from a waterside store where the salesman is probably a sailor himself you may get more practical advice than in one of the big department stores.

You will add to your comfort if you cut up an old towel to wear round your neck as a scarf. This deals with water trickling down the neck.

Whilst not an item of clothing, a good knife is an essential piece of equipment. Only stainless steel will stand up to rust hazards. You will need one with a good blade and one of those spikes you thought were for getting stones out of horses' hoofs. I carry one which also embodies a combined screwdriver and bottle opener. Make a lanyard for it, sling it round your neck and never lend it to anyone else. Oilskins, footwear, knife and personal buoyancy of good quality need not cost more than £12.

If you feel you need to wear something on your head a knitted woollen cap is suitable, but no yachting caps, please – not until you own a boat worthy of one. Two or three summers ago I was talked into packing one when going over to Cowes to sail in a very smart race. On the ferry I noticed that several of the passengers, bound for the same destination, were all wearing this headgear, so I went below and donned my own. As we came alongside Ryde pier another passenger asked me to take his bag ashore and I thought, if you dress like British Railways you must expect to be treated that way. Incidentally, I earned a shilling.

CHAPTER 2

PRACTICE AND THEORY

Rigs – Parts of a Sailing Boat – Rigging and Launching – Points of Sailing – Sailing a Catamaran – Effects of Wind on Sail

IF you have learned to drive a car it is unlikely that you knew what made it go when you started. Your instructor showed you the controls and described their functions, but he did not tell you how a carburettor works, what goes on inside a sparking plug and how the differential operates. Later it may be that you became interested in tuning to get the best performance. At this stage you began to learn some theory and applied your new knowledge to get the best performance.

So it is with a sailing boat. We shall examine practice first and then come to the theory.

Rigs

The square-rigged ship is now only a very beautiful memory. In this sails were fixed to spars called 'yards' which ran at right angles to the masts. The yards could be braced in order to incline them to the wind at different angles in accordance with the point of sailing which the craft was making.

The modern fore-and-aft rig in which the sails are in front of and behind the mast or masts derived from Dutch sailing craft. When Charles II came back to England at the Restoration he brought a yacht with him – the word itself is Dutch in origin. The first race recorded in England was a match between the Royal yacht and another similar vessel at Gravesend, and the King was the winner of a close race against his brother the Duke of York.

The *Botter* is the original form of yacht mentioned above

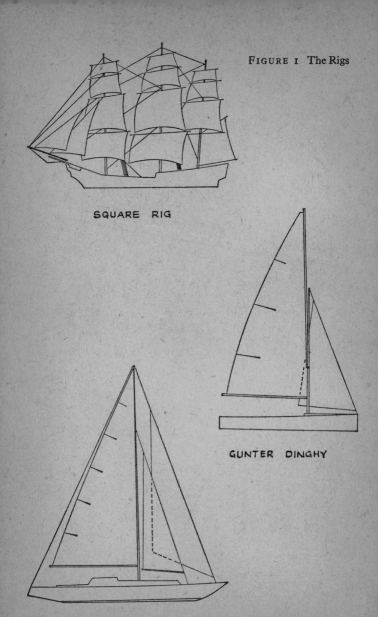

FIGURE I The Rigs

SQUARE RIG

GUNTER DINGHY

CUTTER

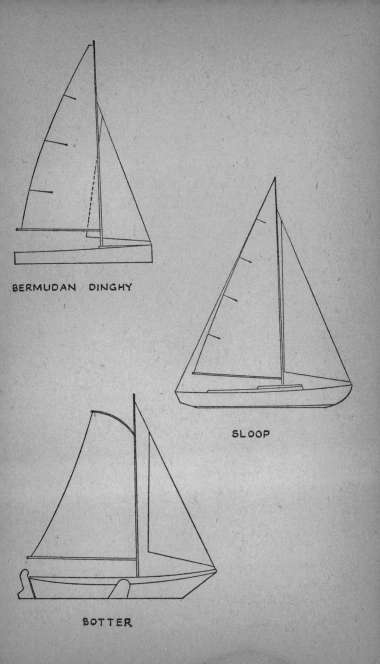

BERMUDAN DINGHY

SLOOP

BOTTER

and it will be seen that the top of the *mainsail*, the larger sail behind the mast, is fixed to a short spar called the *gaff* and the bottom of it to a longer spar, the *boom*. The design has remained practically unaltered over centuries and botters, lemeraks and similar beautiful craft are seen in Dutch waters in great numbers. In time this was developed and the gaff grew a great deal longer. The next type to be evolved was the *Cutter*, which carries more than one foresail which can be rigged in front of the mast. That next to the mast is called the *staysail*, the one next to that the *jib* and occasionally the *flying jib* can still be seen.

The *Sloop* has only one sail in front of the mast and this distinguishes it from the cutter. In both types it was found desirable to add some sail area to the mainsail and so was evolved the *topsail* – difficult to hoist but it filled the triangle between the top of the mast and the gaff. Later still it came to be seen that the topsail was a difficult and unnecessary appendage and from this grew up the one-piece sail and the *Bermudan* rig. A fore-runner of the Bermudan rig is the *Gunter* which gives the advantage of having a sail of the same shape as in the Bermudan rig but since the gaff is in fact an extension of the mast it means that the spars are short and easily stowed within the boat. Although Bermudan is the most popular today designers still produce Gunter-rigged boats, particularly where the aim is to transport them on top of a car. This is because the short mast and spars stow within the boat and so save the overhang of the longer Bermudan mast. Ketches, yawls and schooners are two-masted vessels larger than those which we shall be considering and the distinctions between these are omitted.

Fully 90 per cent of the small boats which sail round the shores of England and on the inland waters are either Bermudan or Gunter-rigged and Figs. 2a and b are general arrangement drawings showing both types together with the names of the principal parts of the boats.

Just as there are languages peculiar to golf, tennis or any other sports so there is a language of boats and sailing. It is

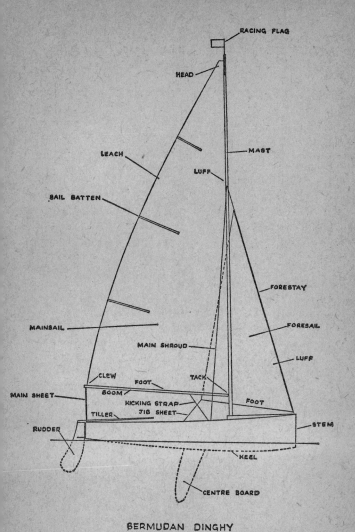

RACING FLAG

HEAD

LEACH

MAST

LUFF

SAIL BATTEN

FORESTAY

FORESAIL

MAINSAIL

MAIN SHROUD

LUFF

CLEW

FOOT

TACK

MAIN SHEET

BOOM

FOOT

KICKING STRAP

TILLER

JIB SHEET

RUDDER

STEM

KEEL

CENTRE BOARD

BERMUDAN DINGHY

FIGURE 2a Bermudan Dinghy

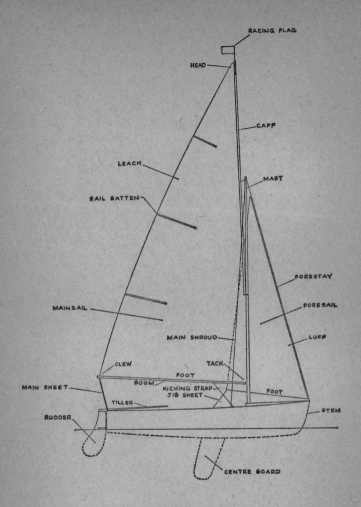

GUNTER DINGHY

FIGURE 2b   Gunter Dinghy

no affectation to learn this language and you will find in Appendix A a very full glossary. In reading this chapter you will find it necessary to make frequent reference to it.

Rigging the Boat

The sails of dinghies and the smaller cruising boats are always taken off their spars, put in a sail-bag and stowed in a dry place after sailing. 'Rigging the Boat' means the whole process of putting on the sails and generally getting ready. Because most small-boat sailors will start with Bermudan or Gunter rig we shall go through the drill of rigging these types. You will have noticed that the main difference between gunter-rig and gaff-rig is the angle made by the gaff with the mast. If you do happen to start your sailing in a boat of less modern rig you will perceive that the principles are very close to each other.

Adopt a standard rigging drill and you will not then be delayed by finding that you have forgotten some essential. The order in which you rig is of no great consequence but I recommend the following:

If afloat on a mooring,

1. Put the rudder on the transom fitting: do not insert the tiller. This is solely to prevent the crew treading on the blade, which can easily be broken or bent.
2. Check that the centre-board or plate is free to move up and down. When a boat takes ground at low tide mud or stones can jam the plate and if you have to sail to windward it must be free to move.
3. Hoist the burgee or, if you are going to race, the square racing flag. And I may as well make it quite clear here and now that to fly a racing flag when you are merely bound for a picnic on the beach is sheer bad manners. The square flag at the masthead implies a request to other helmsmen to ignore the usual Rule of the Road and to keep out of your way.
4. Rig the mainsail ready to hoist.
5. Rig the foresail ready to hoist.

6. Hoist the foresail.
7. Hoist the mainsail.
8. Fix the *tiller* into the *rudder head*.
9. Cast off the mooring.
10. At all times see that sheets are quite free. Never hold the boom if the mainsail is thrashing about – duck your head instead.

If rigging on shore, turn the boat so that it points into the wind or the sails will fill as you try to hoist them. For the rest of the rigging proceed as if on a mooring except that the rudder cannot be put on to the transom fittings until the boat is launched. Try to rig as near the launching point as possible.

When you pull them out of the bag you will find that there is one large and perhaps two smaller sails. The larger is obviously the mainsail and the other one or two are foresails. Dinghies are invariably sloop-rigged and if there are two foresails one of these will be the smaller jib for higher winds and the other a *genoa* for moderate winds : if these have been properly stowed the wire luff of the foresails will be rolled with the *head* innermost and usually owners mark the sail at the *tack* end to show which is which.

Having decided whether you are going to use the larger or smaller foresail replace the other in the sail-bag and set about sorting out the mainsail. If your boat is of Bermudan rig you will have to find the *clew outhaul lanyard*. This is a small rope attached to the clew of the sail and only one corner is so equipped.

Draw the clew of the sail either through the slot cut into the boom for the purpose or along the *track* found on some types – in this case the slides sewn to the sail have to be fed on one by one. At the tack of the mainsail you will find a metal ring (a *cringle*) sewn in and this is secured either by a metal pin passing through a hole drilled in the boom or by a lashing. By passing the outhaul lanyard through a hole drilled in the outer end of the boom the *foot* of the sail is stretched tautly along the boom. In most class boats you will find a clear marking on the boom which shows the limit to which the sail may be stretched. Slip the *battens* into the pockets provided in the leach of the sail.

Should you be rigging a gunter mainsail you may be confused by finding two ropes attached to the corners of the sail. One of these will be for lashing the head of the sail to the outer end of the gaff and it will be near the class insignia and number sewn to the sail.

I wrote earlier that foresails are always stowed with the luff wire rolled and the tack outermost. You must make quite sure that you are shackling the tack and not the head of the sail to the fitting provided at the bottom end of the *forestay*. Get it hoisted upside down and you will be making an international distress signal. Not that anyone will get the lifeboat launched if they see you rigging this way, but if you don't want to have your leg pulled remember that the narrowest corner of the foresail is always the head.

Having shackled on the tack, the leading edge (the luff) is fastened by a series of *hanks* to the forestay, taking care that none are turned over as this might tear the sail. These fittings are of different types, all serving the same purpose. Finally the foresail *sheets* are shackled to the clew cringle and you are ready to shackle on the *halyards* to each sail.

If you look at Fig. 1 you will see that the head of the mainsail goes to the top of the mast in Bermudan rigs, and the main halyard must be that which emerges from the top of the mast. In gunter- or gaff-rigged boats you must find the halyard emerging on the after side of the mast, which will be the main halyard.

Before shackling on each halyard make sure that it is free to run and not foul of the mast or the spreaders.

Haul up the foresail as tautly as possible, taking care that there are no sags along the wire luff and secure the halyard tail to the *cleat*.

Now hoist the mainsail, first of all slacking off the sliding fittings of the *gooseneck* and pushing it up the track provided for it. When the sail is about two-thirds up the mast insert the spiked fitting on the gooseneck into the hole cut into the inner end of the boom and haul on the halyard until the head of the sail has reached the top of the mast. In gunter-rigged boats continue hauling until the gaff has taken up a position in which it is virtually a continuation of the mast.

Make fast the tail of the halyard to the *cleat* provided and pull the gooseneck fitting down its track until the luff of the sail is as taut as possible, securing the gooseneck in this position by the screw provided. Finally slip the button of the kicking-strap into the slot on the underside of the boom, tighten up the *kicking-strap* and your mainsail is ready.

Insert the *tiller* in the *rudder-head* and you are ready to go.

When fastening halyards to cleats do so by making one round turn about the root and two turns round the horns. Jam the halyard under these turns, never knotting it or turning it over.

Coil up the slack of the halyard and hang it on the parent cleat.

All this sounds as if the process is lengthy: in fact one person can get a modern dinghy rigged in under ten minutes. I shall come back to some aspects of rigging under the chapter 'Seamanship' where many of them belong.

Points of Sailing

The different attitudes of a boat and its sails, in relation to the wind, determine the points of sailing. What you must at once recognize is that there is no such thing as a steady wind until well out to sea and even then gusts will vary in strength. In coastal waters, on creeks, in estuaries, on rivers, lakes and reservoirs the wind is constantly varying in strength and direction. The racing helmsman who anticipates these constant changes is usually the first home.

So I am going to start by assuming something that never happens – that a wind is blowing from a constant direction at a constant velocity. Read what follows with frequent reference to Fig. 3.

A boat cannot be pointed at an angle closer to the wind than 45° and to go upwind must do so *close-hauled* in a series

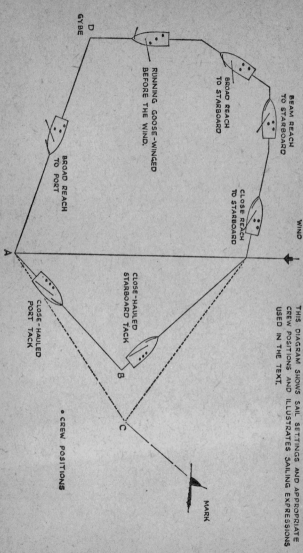

THIS DIAGRAM SHOWS SAIL SETTINGS AND APPROPRIATE CREW POSITIONS AND ILLUSTRATES SAILING EXPRESSIONS USED IN THE TEXT.

WIND

GYBE

D

RUNNING GOOSE-WINGED BEFORE THE WIND.

BROAD REACH TO STARBOARD

BEAM REACH TO STARBOARD

CLOSE REACH TO STARBOARD

BROAD REACH TO PORT

A

CLOSE-HAULED STARBOARD TACK

CLOSE-HAULED PORT TACK

B

C

MARK

• CREW POSITIONS

FIGURE 3 The Points of Sailing

of diagonal *tacks*. The sails are pulled in by their sheets as tightly as possible: if the boat is pointed too close to the wind it loses way. This is called 'pinching' and the first sign of it is a trembling at the luff of the foresail or at the luff of the mainsail if the foresail is not being used.

If a helmsman sailing close-hauled upwind points *off the wind* at an angle greater than 45° he is *bearing away* and obviously needs to make more tacks to reach a given point to windward.

Both pinching and bearing away on a tack are corrected by steering the boat gently back to the correct heading.

A boat should not be pointed at a mark when tacking. The function of the keel is mainly to stop the boat going sideways (making *leeway*) as it goes forward, but it cannot entirely prevent this. Instead of following the solid line from A to B (Fig. 3) it makes good the dotted line to C and if pointed at the mark throughout the tack ends by being badly pinched. This applies in still water but in sailing upwind in a tideway or river the current either advances or retards progress.

Turning the boat off the tack and slightly away from the wind brings it on to a *close reach*. The helmsman has *freed the wind* and it no longer dictates the course to be steered. If the turn away from the wind is continued until it is at a right angle to the boat it is on a *beam reach*. Continuing the turn away brings a *broad reach* and going still farther the wind is finally brought astern.

Notice that each turn away from the wind involves *easing sheets* – letting out sail – until finally with the wind dead astern the mainsail is let out so far that the boom is almost touching the shroud and the foresail is held or boomed out on the opposite side: the boat is now *running goose-winged before the wind*. Often considered to be the fastest and easiest point of sailing, it is neither, and it is here that the beginner is so often caught by the unexpected *gybe*.

The fastest point of sailing is on some form of reach, usually the broad reach. It will vary between boats, even between those of the same design. Many factors come into play

– trimming of the sails, the centre-board settings and weight distribution of the crew. Most modern sailing dinghies are designed to plane, which means that they lift themselves a few inches out of the water, usually on a broad reach. The easing of drag on the boat causes it to accelerate in a cloud of spray and there is no feeling to match it for the dinghy helmsman. Somebody once described his idea of heaven as 'caviar eaten to the sound of trumpets'. Give me a boat getting up on the plane, and holding it.

Now for some detail.

When the boat is turned from one tack to another the operation is termed 'going about' and it invariably involves bringing the bow of the boat over the wind. If the stern is brought over the wind this is 'gybing' and the two are quite different operations.

Going about can only happen if the helm is pushed down and away from the helmsman who normally sits opposite the mainsail, just as gybing can only be brought about by bringing the helm up and towards the helmsman. 'Up' and 'down' in fact mean upwind or downwind but you can think of them as pulling up to you and pushing down and away. There must be no confusion in your mind on these two important points. Nothing is more distressing to your instructor than your question: 'Which way round do I go?', when he has asked you, after hours of patient teaching, to go about at the end of a tack.

Nearing the end of each tack the helmsman sings out: 'Ready about', which is only a warning to the crew – nothing should be done. As he pushes the helm down he calls: 'Lee-oh' and this is the word of command. The foresail is freed and the crew starts to move over the boat: there is no hurry over this and the more slowly the novice helmsman takes it the more likely is he to hit off his new tack accurately. In the first few hours of sailing I always teach helmsmen to give only about 15° of helm when going about and to start the move over the boat only when the boom begins to move. Always face the stern when changing sides: trying to pass the tiller behind your back usually ends with it in your hip pocket. And if you face the stern it is by no means cheating if you like to check the wake of your new tack beginning to make 90° with the wake of the previous tack.

As the foresail fills with wind on the new tack it is sheeted home but an excess of zeal can mean that it is filled aback and the dinghy's bow is pulled back to the original tack. Be quite sure that the bow has passed well over the wind before sheeting in.

The stability and much of the performance of the modern dinghy depends upon the placing of its ballast, the crew itself. Designers have in mind a heel away from the wind of between 10° and 15° except when running, when the boat is upright. More than this makes the keel surface of the centreboard largely ineffective. Whatever the strength of the wind the crew must dispose itself in the boat to achieve this and there are frequent changes in position in gusty winds. A special sense of balance will develop itself and a good crew should never need prompting by the helmsman: get out of your mind that a boat sailing 'on its ear' is going faster than one which is more upright. Typical crew positions are marked on Fig. 3.

In fresh winds helmsman and crew will be sitting out, feet tucked under the toestraps, so as to put as much weight outboard to windward as possible. Most modern dinghies have a hinged extension to the tiller so that the helmsman can also sit out on the side deck. When the wind gusts the helmsman lets a little main sheet run out to spill wind and centralizes the tiller which he will have pulled slightly up to weather on the first impact of the wind increase to prevent the boat turning up into wind. The foresail is not eased under any but the most abnormal circumstances when a beginner should not be sailing in any case.

I notice that many beginners tend to pull on everything when hit by a gust. This merely serves to increase the heel and the sense of insecurity which may accompany it. In times of stress in a boat a general rule is to relax on the controls.

In lighter winds sitting out is not only unnecessary but

will also slow the boat if the mast is heeled over to windward.

Only by intense concentration will you learn to take the boat really well to windward. The eye will soon discern the faint tremble of the foresail luff which precedes the pinch and excessive heel of the boat will indicate bearing away on the tack. Your aim must be to acquire a control at once gentle and firm, best defined as 'hands for a boat'.

Never hold sheet and tiller in the same hand unless you have to free a hand for some essential purpose. The tiller is always held by the hand nearest to it and the main sheet by the other: when going about make the change of hands as you go over the boat. Whilst changing tack smartly is desirable remember that a violent thrust away of the tiller can stop the boat dead. A more gentle easing round keeps way on and gives more time to get over the boat. By all means speed up as experience grows but take it easy in the first days and concentrate on hitting off the new tack with absolute accuracy.

I have written above that there is nothing constant about the speed and direction of the wind and this must never be forgotten. Nothing is more disconcerting to the beginner than to have the boat at one moment sailing well on a tack, at the next to have it losing way with a flapping foresail.

The first reaction to this is usually that some helming error has been made but it is more likely that there has been a wind shift which has brought it more ahead of the boat. There is only one remedy: the tiller must be brought gently up until the foresail fills again and the boat resumes tack. You must remember that once the boat is brought to the new heading a small contrary movement of the tiller is needed to check the swing.

A wind-shift when on a close reach, for example, can turn this point of sailing into a tack. If the boat is sailing at anything more than 45° with the wind, refilling a pinching foresail is not effected by turning away from the wind but by hardening sheets. Only when close-hauled is the pinch corrected by turning the whole boat. At first some difficulty may be found in distinguishing between wind shifts and decreases in strength.

Judging the direction of the wind presents a difficulty to the beginner. Many pin their faith to the burgee at the top of the mast or to tell-tales fixed to the shrouds. These do not show the true direction except when the boat is on a mooring or running before the wind. On all other points of sailing they show only the apparent direction compounded of the true wind and the wind which the boat makes from its own movement.

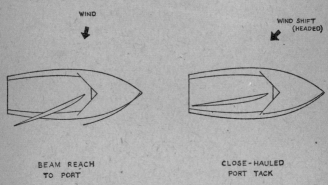

FIGURE 4 Countering a wind shift

Learn to judge the direction of the true wind from the ripples on the water. Keep a weather eye cocked to windward to spot the dark catspaws of approaching gusts. Do nothing to anticipate their effect for they may never reach you. But be ready.

Above all sail on the wind which is blowing where you are. Never try to point parallel with another boat. Even on open waters the wind may vary between two boats only a few yards apart.

Some effects of wind movements are shown in Fig. 4.

As soon as the heading of the boat is away from the wind at more than 45° it begins to *sail free*. Movements of the crew are adjusted to the new equilibrium. Sheets are eased but not so far that sails flap or tremble at the luffs. The centreboard or dagger plate is brought up slightly, for with each turn away from wind less is required until no keel surface at all is required when running unless the boat shows a tendency to roll. Enough keel to check this may then be lowered.

The first sign that successive turns away from wind are bringing the boat to the run position is that the foresail, which should have been kept in about the same plane as the mainsail, will fall in and refuse to fill. It is then brought across the boat to the goose-wing position and any further turn away from wind will bring the gybe very near. The helmsman will watch the boom very closely and any tendency for it to lift or swing over can be checked by a slight push down of the tiller.

All beginners seem to have heard horrible tales of gybing and one even reads the advice that beginners should never attempt it. This is on a level with recommending that a car should never be driven in reverse. It is a manoeuvre just like any other and if it is called for, it is executed. A helmsman may be in trouble if the boat gybes him instead of him gybing the boat. Get the drill right and there is nothing to it.

Look again at Fig. 3 and you will see that the preponderance of crew weight is now on the lee side of the boat which will become the weather side when the boom is brought over. The helmsman gives the crew the warning: 'Stand by to gybe.' As he draws the helm slightly up to effect it he calls: 'Gybe-oh' and one of the crew pulls the boom over as the bow comes round. As the boom swings the helmsman must apply check tiller to prevent the boat continuing to swing round until it is pointing up into wind.

The dinghy gybe is best effected *all-standing* without the hauling in and subsequent rapid easing off of the mainsheet which applies to the larger keel boats.

Should you buy a boat which includes a spinnaker in the suit of sails, do not be in a hurry to use it. Your best course will be to persuade a more experienced helmsman to show you

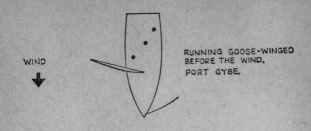

WIND

RUNNING GOOSE-WINGED
BEFORE THE WIND.
PORT GYBE.

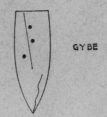

GYBE

RUNNING GOOSE-WINGED
BEFORE THE WIND.
STARBOARD GYBE

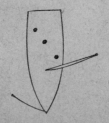

FIGURE 5A Gybing: note the crew positions

how to handle the sail, for you may otherwise run the risk of tearing the light fabric as well as getting into some confusing situations.

If you lay out the sail on the ground you will find that it is cut so that the wind fills it out into a semi-spherical shape. This means that with the wind dead aft it does a good job of pushing the boat along. If the boat is turned or the wind shifts to come more from the quarter or abeam, the spinnaker boom has to be eased off until the sail begins to function as a very large foresail. The semi-spherical shape makes it difficult to keep the sail full of wind and the large area forward of the mast may unbalance the steering. When this becomes apparent (preferably a little before) the spinnaker must come down without any hitches: a collapsed spinnaker, insufficiently smothered, has a fiendish way of getting into the water, under the boat and wrapped round the centreboard in no time at all.

I have not written this to put you off using a spinnaker but to underline the fact that you must know what you are about.

If you must try it by yourself, pick a day and a situation when you have an unencumbered downwind sail of at least a mile ahead of you and not more than Force 3 wind behind you.

The spinnaker must be prepared and stowed in a sailbag or a box so that it is not twisted. The three corners of the sail must be arranged so as to be at the top of the container and it will be found that the bottom starboard corner has green webbing stitched to it, the port corner, red webbing. The head of the sail has corresponding green and red webbing at the apex.

It must be remembered that the spinnaker is held to the mast only by the halyard at the head, the rest of the sail ballooning in the wind and controlled by ropes running to the two bottom corners. In preparing to hoist you must visualize how everything will work out when you have done so.

Let us suppose that you have started to sail downwind on

a port gybe, which means that the mainsail is boomed out over
the starboard side and that the spinnaker will be boomed out
over the port side.

Two ropes control the spinnaker at the bottom edge: the

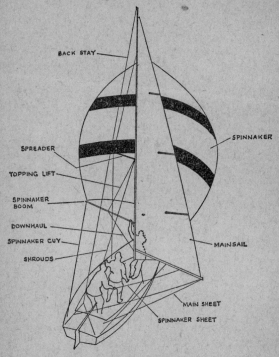

BACK STAY

SPINNAKER

SPREADER

TOPPING LIFT

SPINNAKER
BOOM

DOWNHAUL

SPINNAKER GUY

SHROUDS

MAINSAIL

MAIN SHEET

SPINNAKER SHEET

FIGURE 5B

guy which connects to the corner of the sail which is fixed
to the outer end of the spinnaker boom and the *sheet* which
controls the remaining free corner. On this port gybe the
guy will be on the port side and the sheet on the starboard
side. Had you been sailing gybed to starboard the same ropes
would have exchanged their functions and descriptions.

You will start by clipping the guy to the port (red webbing) corner of the sail; clip outer end of the spinnaker boom to the same corner and the inner end to the fitting on the forward side of the mast; lead the sheet *outside* the forestay and clip it to the starboard (green webbing) corner of the sail; clip the halyard to the head (red and green webbing) and hoist away. As soon as the spinnaker is up get the foresail down and bundled up so that it will not flap free.

Provided that the helmsman has not become so immersed in the intricacies of the manoeuvre that he has wandered off course and that all goes well with the hoisting, some play on guy and sheet will fill the spinnaker. On your first essay do not try to carry the sail too long. Get it down well before you have to change direction.

Use of the spinnaker is simple enough when you know enough and much depends on the preparations before hoisting. But perhaps you see my point in suggesting that you may need some expert advice.

Catamarans

Most of the established designs of catamaran are easy to sail once it is recognized that they differ in handling characteristics from conventional dinghies. Very fast off the wind, they do not point so well or sail fast on the tack. Going about frequently calls for the backing of the foresail (see Chapter 3 – 'Seamanship') to assist in getting the bow over the wind.

Nor are catamarans uncapsizeable. Given the conditions any small boat can be capsized and it can be a considerable problem to right a multi-hulled vessel.

The heel away from the wind of a conventional dinghy relieves strains on rigging and mast. The resistance to heeling in catamarans imposes heavy loads on shrouds and forestay and these must always be kept under close inspection for signs of weakness. A parted shroud or faulty rigging-screw can cost a mast.

All that I have written about catamarans applies equally to trimarans. You will always meet the small boat man who cannot stand them, probably because he has never sailed one. It must be remembered that multi-hulled craft occupy at least twice the space of a conventional dinghy when parked or moored and for this reason some clubs are unhappy over accepting new members who propose to sail one.

Some builders are at fault in representing the catamaran or the trimaran as the simple answer to easy sailing. There are no substitutes for practical tuition, concentration and practice. In your early days you will make many mistakes. Learn from them, be patient with yourself (and your crew) and your new skills will grow at a remarkable rate.

The Effect of Wind on Sails

Why a boat should be able to sail towards the wind invariably baffles the beginner who knows nothing of the subject. The fact is that sailors were dealing in practical aerodynamics long before the term was coined. Sails are now tested in wind tunnels and their cutting and shaping is an exact science. If you have any small knowledge of aerodynamics you will soon appreciate that the mainsail functions exactly like the wing of an aircraft but in a different plane – thrusting instead of lifting.

Wind pressure on the windward side of a sail passes over its curve and has a tendency to drive the boat both ahead and sideways. Hence the keel surface is essential when tacking. But wind passing over the lee side of a sail travels faster than the flow over the windward side and this creates a partial vacuum which literally sucks the boat to windward, so long as it is not headed closer to wind than 45°. This lee side suction is twice as powerful as the thrust from the windward side of the sail. If the flow of wind over the lee side of the sail is accelerated the boat goes much faster to windward and this vital stepping-up is achieved by the slot effect between foresail and mainsail (Fig. 6). Forced into a narrowing funnel, the wind increases the partial vacuum until the boat reaches the maximum windward thrust.

The foresail *fairleads* are positioned so that when the sail is sheeted home hard on the tack the maximum slot effect is reached. Wind acceleration is important not only when tacking but on every point of sailing except running; here the mainsail ceases to act as a thrusting wing and becomes a less efficient parachute. For this reason I wrote earlier that running before the wind is the slowest point of sailing. To overcome this a spinnaker is sometimes set on the run but is rarely found in dinghies which beginners are likely to sail.

All too often the beginner left in charge of the foresail pulls it in hard irrespective of the point of sailing. Ideally the curve of the foresail is in about the same plane as that of the main. If it is sheeted in too hard the wind flow bounces off it

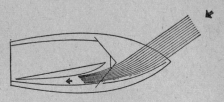

FIGURE 6   Ideal slot effect

into the partial vacuum area, destroying it, backwinding the mainsail and slowing the boat (Fig. 7).

The shape of the mainsail is a factor of great importance. When it leaves the sailmaker it has been accurately cut and sewn. The treatment of the sail in the early days can cause it to lose its designed contour and whilst the terylene sails that are now in general use need less careful stretching than sailcloth, stretching in gentle winds on the first two occasions is advisable.

Ideally the best shape for a mainsail is a gentle curve away from the luff tapering off to a flattening toward the *leech*. In strong winds the boat will go best to windward if the sail is stretched as tautly as possible in the luff and *along the foot*. This flattens the sail, increases ability to sail close to the wind. In light winds a fuller curve drives the boat better and the sail is less tightly stretched at luff and foot.

Foresails are usually designed so that the *mitre* (a diagonal seam running from the clew towards the luff) continues the line of the sheet up from the fairlead. It is now being found that expense can be avoided in terylene sails cut to an approximate right angle at the clew because of the great strength of the cloth, and the mitre seam is sometimes absent. In designing the boat the appropriate position of the fairlead will have been worked out but adjustments of this may well vary with individual sails. A fairlead is sometimes set in a sliding track to permit of adjustment.

A quick method of checking that the foresail is properly shaped by the sheet is to see that the whole length of the luff flutters as the boat is pointed into wind.

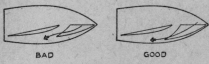

BAD   GOOD

FIGURE 7 Poor slot effect

Modern dinghies usually need adjustments of standing rigging to obtain the best balance. It should be possible to sail the boat on a tack in a reasonably steady wind with the tiller in a central position. Gusts of wind will mean the temporary application of weather helm – pulling the tiller slightly up to keep the boat on course and to check its inbuilt tendency to head up into wind. If at all times weather helm is necessary this indicates that the mast is raked too far aft. A tightening of the forestay and a corresponding slackening of each shroud will improve the balance.

If a permanent lee helm is needed to hold the boat on course the mast must be raked farther aft. This is a condition which should be dealt with at once. A boat which is unable to turn up into wind when a gust is met can be dangerous to sail.

Excessive weather or lee helm drastically reduces the speed

of a boat through the water. The drag imposed by the rudder can cut the speed by 20 per cent or more. There are various temporary expedients which can slightly better these faults in balance but I do not propose to examine them. By far the best course is to adjust the rigging and by trial and error arrive at having a well-balanced boat.

These are the basics of theory and a much wider knowledge will be needed as experience grows. After you have done some sailing read one of the specialist books on the subject: *Dinghy Racing* (Ian Proctor) is a good example. The sailing magazines publish many articles and readers' letters on the fascinating theme of how to make a good boat even better by the application of theory to practice.

CHAPTER 3.

SEAMANSHIP

Leaving a Mooring – Leaving the Shore – Returning to a Mooring – Returning to the Shore – Going Aground – Reefing – Nursing – Sea Anchors – Dead Downwind – Stern Way – Rescue – Handling a Tender

THE art of seamanship is that of handling a vessel under all conditions of sea and wind. It ranges from such simple matters as a neat arrival on a mooring to the salvage of another vessel in a high wind. Because it calls for resource and ingenuity a high degree of proficiency in seamanship is one of the most satisfying attainments. Just as a boxer rides a punch, so helmsman and crew combine the run of the sea and wind with the capabilities of the boat. To ignore these factors spells failure.

Leaving a Mooring

At first sight there would appear to be no problem: just get up the sails, cast off and go. In fact quite a lot can go wrong.

The crew will have gone out to the mooring in a tender which is to be left behind unless you are going to tow it astern of a keel boat. In the latter case all that has to be done is to attach the tender's painter to a cleat on the stern after the crew is on board. Not too long a towline, for a tender can easily wrap itself round a mooring chain if you have to tack through a crowded anchorage.

If the tender is to be left behind on the mooring, bring up on the same side of your sailing boat as the mooring chain. By this is meant that on one side of the forestay and very close to it will be found a fairlead through which passes the mooring chain. The tender must be brought up to this same side. When the crew is aboard tie the painter of the tender through any convenient link of the mooring chain near the rope strop connecting chain and mooring buoy. Be sure that the painter is outside the shrouds and that both chain and painter are underneath the foresail sheets. Fail in this and you will still be connected to the mooring when trying to sail off.

Now get sails up, taking particular care that sheets are quite free to run. Otherwise the boat will sail around the mooring before you are ready to go.

If you are about to sail from a mooring and the chain leads through a fairlead on the starboard side of the forestay you will have to leave on starboard tack so as to clear the moored tender. You will have fewer problems if you are sailing a dinghy rather than a keel boat because the dinghy always swings head to wind on a mooring whilst a keel boat is more likely to be swinging with the tide: we shall deal with keel boats later.

Put the mooring buoy into the tender: make a last check to see that you are going to be clear when the mooring is cast off. Have your crew hold the foresail out to starboard by the clew so that it fills aback and pushes the bow round to port. As the mainsail fills give the word to let go chain and you are away.

If you are in a keel boat swinging to the tide you will be able to follow the same drill if wind and tide are substantially coming from the same direction. If on balance the wind and tide are coming from opposite directions you will have to leave under foresail alone, turning up into wind and getting up the mainsail as soon as you have sufficient space in which to manoeuvre.

Leaving the Shore

Your problems will be fewest if your departure is from a windward shore. All that is required is to launch the dinghy from its trolley with the sails set and all sheets free to run. One member of the crew must hold the boat by the bow whilst the remainder get aboard. When the rudder is shipped and the tiller in position the man at the bow pushes it round so that the sails fill and scrambles aboard. The helmsman must ensure that the mainsail is not hauled in too tightly at the start or the boat will tend to run up into wind before it has gathered way and ground again on the shore.

If the wind is blowing on to the shore it may be that launching from a slightly different point may ease the difficulties. Few shores are without indentations or irregularities which may be helpful by bringing the wind to an easier angle.

Should the shore run in a straight line there is nothing for it save for one crew member to get into the water holding the bow. The launching trolley is less easy to withdraw but if your boat is light and your crew strong enough the solution may be to carry it a couple of yards. Never drag a dinghy over a beach or even over sand or mud. The first will score the bottom and the latter force sand or mud into the centreboard casing.

Once the dinghy is afloat as much centreboard as possible must be lowered, the bowman pushes the head of the boat off the wind and scrambles aboard as she gathers way. As the water gets deeper more centreboard and rudder blade are lowered. To sail to windward with the rudder blade in the 'up' position imposes unfair strains on the rudder hood and cheeks.

Returning to a Mooring

I notice that beginners always feel that some point of honour is involved if they fail to pick up the mooring at the first attempt. It is far better to make a dummy run – two or three if you wish – than to get into irons and drift on to another moored boat. This happens because the helmsman tries to sail the boat closer to the wind than is possible. Once it becomes clear from the fluttering of the sails that way is being lost, do not hesitate to go about, make two very short tacks and have another try.

Remember that conditions are never identical and that no rule of thumb can apply. Don't get flustered because fellow

members of your club are watching; they've all made a mess
of it in their time.

The perfect approach to a mooring is one which keeps way
on the boat – just – until the moment when the buoy is picked
up. If it is too fast some unfortunate risks having his arms

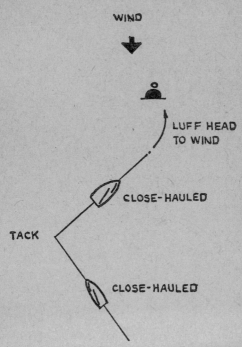

FIGURE 8 Approach to a windward mooring

pulled out at the sockets: too slow and the helmsman does
not have enough steerage way. Nor is the solution to get up to
windward of the buoy and drift on to it. The boat must be
steered to the mooring, which must always, without any exception, be picked up at the bow.

Once again the problems are fewest for the dinghy helmsman. His boat is only slightly affected by the run of the tide and if the mooring has deep water all round it the best approach is to come up to the buoy on a tack, easing sheets to reduce speed as he gets near, turning up into wind at the moment of picking up. If the buoy is missed for any reason then there is only one course: harden the sheets, get some way on the boat again and have another try.

Your first attempts at picking up a mooring should always be made when there is plenty of deep water in which to

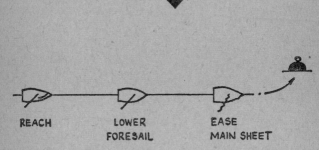

WIND

REACH   LOWER   EASE
            FORESAIL   MAIN SHEET

FIGURE 9   Approach to mooring on a beam reach

manoeuvre round the buoy. All kinds of complications can arise if a missed mooring can mean going aground on a falling tide.

You will not want to miss hours of sailing by returning at the top of the tide. Nor is it likely that you will get a dinghy mooring where your boat is always afloat at all states of the tide.

This means that the planning of your sail and in particular the time for returning to moorings must relate to the conditions of the day. Some will hold that this has nothing to do with seamanship. I maintain that the helmsman who misses the tide because of bad planning is a poor seaman.

Let us suppose that you have mastered the simple approach to windward and consider some of the more difficult cases.

Figure 9 shows the mooring near shallow water and the wind permitting an approach on a beam reach. Remember that this is one of the fastest points of sailing and provided

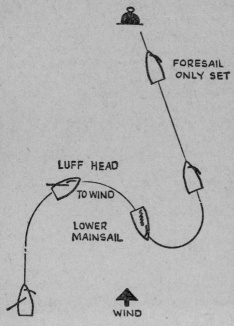

FIGURE 10 Approach to a leeward mooring

that your boat handles satisfactorily under mainsail alone, reduce speed by getting the foresail down. I make a practice of this when approaching a buoy to windward or on a beam reach because it is so much easier to pick it up without the encumbrance of a flapping foresail. And get it down in good time: leave it until the last moment and something always jambs.

Once again the aim is to approach the buoy at the minimum of steerage way. All that has to be done is to ease the mainsheet, pushing out the boom to spill wind if necessary, and sail quietly up to the mooring.

Figure 10 illustrates a more complicated problem. Here the wind direction compels an approach towards shallows to leeward. Unless a tide is running strongly against you or the wind is very light indeed any approach under full sail is impossible.

The solution is to turn the boat up into wind, get the mainsail down smartly and sail up to the mooring under foresail alone. Unless the following wind is light enough to allow the mainsail to be sheeted in before lowering, do not attempt to get it down when it is full of wind. By doing so you risk tearing the sail, quite aside from displaying bad seamanship.

In a high wind the boat may well be going over the ground too fast under the foresail, in which case it must come down and you must come up to the buoy under the bare pole. The windage on a mast is far more than you imagine. Do not forget that the crew constitutes windage if all members stand up, as so frequently seems to happen when the inexperienced try to pick up a mooring in a blow.

It must not be forgotten that an approach of this kind allows of one chance only. If the buoy is missed at the first attempt grounding on the shallows is almost inevitable. The bowman must do his best to guide the helmsman and at the same time to keep out of his line of sight. In a sailing dinghy of sufficient size and stability he can best do this by lying flat on his face on the foredeck.

Approaches to a buoy lying to leeward by a keel boat entail a fair knowledge of his craft by the helmsman. If she tends to be tide-rode rather than wind-rode she will then swing parallel with other craft lying moored near by. But a shallow-draught keel boat may well tend to behave like a dinghy in swinging to the wind rather than to the tide.

Some points to remember about picking up moorings:

1. If your approach (from windward and with room to

manoeuvre, of course) is too fast, abandon it and try again.

2. Always pick up the buoy at the bow, get the chain through the bow fairlead and secured to the mooring cleat as quickly as possible.

3. The bowman *must* let the helmsman know when he has caught the buoy and secured the chain.

4. As soon as the mooring chain is secured sail must come down at once. Nothing looks worse, or is worse for the mooring, than to be secured to it and sailing in circles around it.

Returning to the Shore

If you have any choice in the matter always try to bring your boat to a windward shore. Your procedure then will be exactly the same as coming up to a mooring buoy – coming in on a tack with the sheets eased and pointing up into wind to reduce speed as the boat grounds. As you come into the shallower water the centreboard and rudder-blade must be raised, the former in stages and coming to the fully up position only as you point into wind just before grounding. If the centreboard is fully raised too early the boat will make excessive leeway to the detriment of other boats on a popular beach.

Should you be returning to your base all that you will have to do is to float your dinghy on to the launching trolley and haul her up. If you are landing for a picnic you must consider whether the tide is rising or falling. A strong enough crew and a light boat means that she can be carried to the water for re-launching if the tide is ebbing.

Most probably you will elect to use the anchor. See that it is well trodden in and be generous in the scope of the *warp* you allow. The longer it is the better the anchor will hold.

If you have to return to a lee shore the same procedure applies as for picking up a buoy to leeward – turn up into wind, drop the mainsail and come in on the foresail. At all costs avoid ramming the beach at the speed of an express train.

Should you elect to picnic on a lee shore you must think in advance about getting off again. The light boat can be carried up the beach and relaunched but the heavier boat should be kept afloat.

This is best effected by sailing boldly up to the beach and turning up into wind fairly sharply. The sails will flap and if the boat is kept pointing into the eye of the wind she will start going astern very slowly. At this moment the anchor is thrown out well ahead, sails are lowered and stowed, and the rudder and tiller are unshipped and stowed. If the anchor warp is now paid out it will be possible to land off the stern. Sailing off is effected by hoisting sail and hauling in the anchor warp smartly.

Nobody lands on a lee shore for choice, or ought not to. With the rise or fall of the tide – and it is bound to be doing one or the other – frequent adjustments of the anchor-warp are needed. In my own harbour dinghy sailors flock like sheep to a popular sandy beach which gives a windward shore with the usually prevailing winds. They still go there when the wind blows onshore and only a half-mile away opposite is another delightful and empty beach giving a windward shore. A good seaman never does anything the hard way.

Going Aground

The dinghy helmsman usually runs aground when he has prolonged a tack by just those few yards too much. If the tide is rising he has time to think. Should it be falling there is no time to lose.

The immediate reaction when the centreboard hits the bottom must be to go about and go into deeper water. Since the tip of the centreboard itself may be stuck in sand or mud it must be raised sufficiently to free it. Turning the boat without taking this precaution may break or bend the centreboard. But the centreboard must not be brought fully up, for the boat will not go about without any keel surface and will only drift sideways into ever shallowing water.

If the boat has lost all steerage way the foresail may be held out aback so that the bow is pushed round on to the new tack away from the shallows. Or somebody gets over the side and

pushes the boat round and this may well be the best course if
you have gone aground on a falling tide when water recedes
with every minute of debate.

Should it not be possible to get the bow round on to the

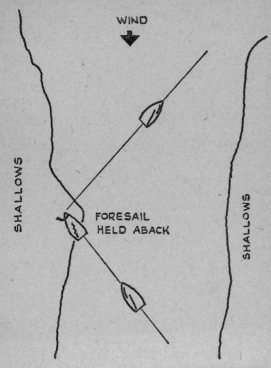

FIGURE 11 Going aground and getting off

new tack it may be expedient to gybe off. In attempting this
you must be bold in your execution of the manoeuvre, for
you will have only a little space in which to move.

Having gone on to the shoal with the centreboard down
this will mean that there is in fact some three feet of water
under your boat, the depth decreasing nearer the shore.

The foresail is sheeted hard in and the mainsheet fully eased by pushing on the boom. The lifting rudder is hoisted up until only a few inches are immersed, the helm is pulled and held hard up and the centreboard is fully raised. The

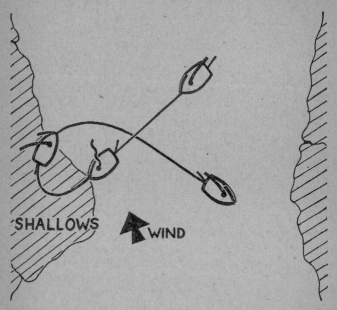

FIGURE 12 Gybing off after going aground

boat should immediately turn off wind until the mainsail gybes and you can then sail off into the deeper water. When there is enough depth centreboard and rudder are lowered and your sail continues. But don't hold the next tack quite so long.

Keel boats are not such an easy proposition. Gybing off

cannot be attempted because the keel cannot be raised. I have seen the devoted crews of smaller keel boats up to their shoulders in the water pushing the bows off but this may well be impossible on a mud bottom.

Sheets must be eased at once and the sails allowed to flap. If they remain sheeted in hard they are only driving the keel deeper into the shoal. Keel boats should always have a main (*bower*) anchor and a lighter (*kedge*) anchor. One of the uses of the latter is in kedging off a shoal and it should at once be lowered into the dinghy with its warp and rowed out as far as possible for dropping into deep water. The after end of the keel draws most water and it may well help to get the weight of the crew into the bow as they try to haul off. If there is an auxiliary motor it may help to run it reverse, but do not pin your faith to this. The propellor is only about half effective in reverse gear.

If you have no tender in tow and no friendly power craft drawing less water to offer to pluck you off, then you must wait for the tide to float you. And it may be a long wait if you have gone aground on a falling tide.

Reefing

When winds are strong it is necessary to reduce the sail area by reefing. If this is not done it is usually still possible to sail the boat while wind is spilled from the mainsail but it is far more comfortable to reef. Remember that it is best to reef before you leave the shore or mooring. Shaking out a reef is quickly done.

In the older gaff-rigged types you will find sewn into the mainsail one, two or even three rows of reefing-points — strings on either side of the sail. Very slightly above them and sewn into the luff and leach are cringles, which are the important parts when it comes to reefing. With the sail only partly hoisted and the boat headed into wind, the two cringles are lashed down to the boom and the reefing points tied with a reef knot (Fig. 13). When shaking out the reef the points must be untied before letting go the cringle lashings, otherwise the sail may easily tear. After the reef is discarded the sail must be fully hoisted again.

It is rare to come across a reefing foresail but the method is the same – lash down the cringles and then tie the points. More usually a smaller foresail is used in strong winds.

In the modern rigs the mainsail area is reduced by rolling it round the boom, the hoisting halyard being slacked off to allow of this. Sometimes the rotation of the boom is effected by using a ratchet gear which locks it in position but this is usually found in craft of $2\frac{1}{2}$ tons upwards. In sailing dinghies

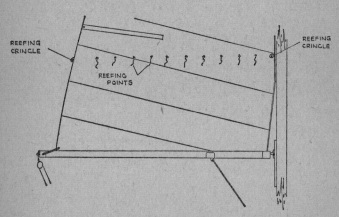

FIGURE 13 Reefing with cringles and points

the boom can be rotated if it is withdrawn from the gooseneck, which is square in section so that it will lock the boom in position when the gooseneck is thrust into it.

Whatever the type of fitting for reefing, the sail must be rolled round the boom with as few wrinkles or creases as possible.

I have already stressed the importance of the kicking-strap and at no time is it more useful than in a high wind. Where reefing is effected by rolling the mainsail round the boom the button fitment must be removed and so the kicking-strap is out of action. There are various devices which allow the mainsail to be reefed whilst retaining the kicking-strap.

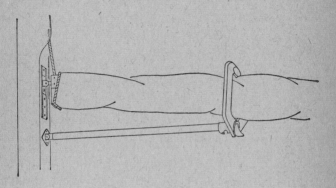

FIGURE 14 'Lewmar' patent reefing claw

One example is the reefing-claw made by Lewmar Marine Ltd. and illustrated at Fig. 14. The shaft fits on to its own gooseneck so that it can move with the boom and the claws can be opened by releasing the catch. Another method is to roll in with the sail a piece of webbing fitted with a rope tail to act as the kicking-strap. This is cheap and effective but is said by some to distort the shape of the sail.

Nursing

Any sailing boat driven hard in heavy weather becomes difficult to hold, particularly if you have been caught un-reefed in a sudden blow. In big seas a dinghy may ship water

over the sides and will certainly do so from the sheets of
spray as each wave is struck. These are the conditions when a
boat must be nursed.

If the boat is taken more slowly through the water it will
put less strain on the gear and the crew will be much more
comfortable and dry. All that need be done is to spill wind
from the mainsail by easing sheet. It may even be expedient to
turn the bow to meet the larger waves but steerage way must
always be retained. A sailing boat is very vulnerable in irons
in a wild sea.

You may notice that less water is shipped on one tack than
upon the other. If the wind allows of it make short tacks on the
uncomfortable leg, longer tacks on the drier leg. Try to work
under any convenient lee which presents itself. You will not
be able to anchor in broken water but try to get some reefs in
as soon as possible.

Never allow water to accumulate in the boat. One crew
member must be put to baling and all must do their best to
sit the boat upright.

The main responsibility for nursing a boat through a chop
lies with the helmsman and within this brief section it is not
possible to examine all the different circumstances and conditions which may arise. Probably the best summary is in the
words : 'Take it easy and don't over-drive her.'

Sea Anchors

Among the items later listed as the equipment of keel boat
yachts is a sea anchor. This takes the form of a canvas cone
open at both ends. From the wider end is rigged a bridle to
which a warp may be attached and the purpose of it is to hold
the boat up to weather in gale conditions. Tidal movement
may thrust the vessel on to a lee shore but given some sea-room
a yacht can ride out very heavy weather.

A sea anchor is not among the equipment normally carried
in a sailing dinghy although helmsmen of the calibre of Frank
Dye will do so when setting out on long voyages. Dye has
several times sailed his 16-ft Wayfarer across the North Sea

and was on one occasion caught in a Force 8 blow. He lowered his mast in the tabernacle and rode out the gale lying to the sea anchor.

The beginner ought not to be out at all in the open sea if there is any risk of winds such as this developing. An emergency sea anchor can be devised by fixing a rope cage round

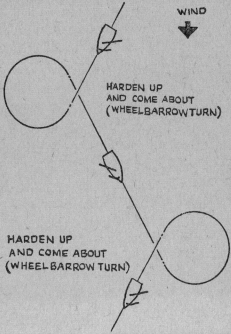

WIND

HARDEN UP
AND COME ABOUT
(WHEELBARROW TURN)

HARDEN UP
AND COME ABOUT
(WHEELBARROW TURN)

FIGURE 15 Tacking downwind

a bucket. The ordinary handle will probably not hold. A spare sail loosely bundled and tightly lashed can also serve.

Dead Downwind

I have earlier made the point that running before the wind is not the easiest point of sailing. A dead run before a heavy wind brings with it constant anxiety about an unplanned gybe or broaching broadside to the waves. Under pressure on the mainsail the vessel fights to point up into wind and an over-correction on the helm may bring the gybe you want to avoid.

If you have to sail dead downwind in a blow, either do so in a series of broad reaches linking each with the next by a 'wheelbarrow turn' or sail under the foresail alone. Even under the latter circumstances you may find that your craft is running down the waves so fast that she buries her bow and ships water. In a dinghy the weight of the crew must be brought aft.

In either a dinghy or a keel boat the wild plunge down the waves can be slowed by trailing a long warp over the stern.

Stern Way

Many clubs organize seamanship races which bring helmsmen face to face with problems they have never before met. This kind of race is a splendid thing and more clubs might well think about it. In one such annual event helmsmen have to cross both the start and finish lines making stern way.

In your earlier days you will be bound to have found yourself through some misjudgment to be pointing up into wind in a stationary boat. Your first reaction will be to waggle the tiller about to try to get the boat to do *something*. The usual result of this is that the boat begins to move slowly backwards.

A boat will answer the helm so long as it is moving through the water either ahead or astern. All that pump-handling the tiller does is to keep her pointing head to wind. If she starts to go astern the rudder still guides the boat, but in the opposite direction from the normal.

Suppose that you are making stern way and wish to get sailing again on a port tack. Push the tiller hard down to starboard, hold it there until the sails begin to fill as you make 45° with the wind, and you are off again. The tiller is centralized, of course, as the boat gathers forward way.

There are many situations where the deliberate use of stern

way is called for. Practise it: you will find it fascinating and
extremely useful at times.

Rescue

I never go on a pier if I can help it because I always
wonder what on earth I should do if I had to rescue a drowning
child.

The time will inevitably come in your sailing career when
you are helming the only boat anywhere near a capsize. You
will feel obliged to do something about it. The first thing to
do is to find out whether the capsized crew want any help:
they may be racing in an event in which some points are
scored for finishing and outside help disqualifies. (I know one
mother who bought her children a Cadet and had the word
'Help' painted in orange letters on the bottom: her mutinous
young painted it over after a week.)

If the capsized dinghy is drifting towards a lee shore where
it will soon ground there is probably not much you can do
unless the crew are not wearing personal buoyancy and look
like drowning. If the boat can be got to a firm lee shore the
crew should be able to right it and get sailing again without
your help unless some vital piece of gear has been broken in
the capsize. Perhaps the best thing you can do is to sail about
near by until it is clear that the situation is under control.

If you judge that a rescue must be attempted it must
always come from a windward direction. Most probably the
capsize will have occurred in a flurry of wind and this means
that with any luck the mast will be lying in the water pointing
down to the lee.

Sail away a little, get the foresail down and tie it round the
forestay with the sheets to prevent it flapping. Get the anchor
ready and see that there is plenty of warp to pay out. Shortly
it is going to have to hold two boats and the longer the scope
you can give the better it will hold. Another warp will have to
be available in the stern of your boat for casting to the capsize.

Now sail up from slightly downwind and turn up into wind
so that both boats line up with the wind direction, finishing as

close as you can to the capsize. This is where you have to act quickly.

Your crew lets go anchor and pays out the warp. Stopping only to see that your mainsheet is quite free, cast a warp to the capsize in the hope that one of the crew will attach it quickly to some part of his boat. No time must be lost because the capsize will be moving away from you as the wind catches the bottom of the boat. When you are sure that the anchor is holding both boats get the mainsail down.

If the capsized crew want to come aboard your boat get them in over the transom. This is easier and obviates the risk of another capsize happening to you. Make a loop out of a piece of rope – the end of the mainsheet will do – to serve as a foothold and the scramble aboard is simple enough.

Provided that the capsized dinghy has proper buoyancy it can be righted and baled out in the normal fashion. If it has none it will probably have to be left on its anchor in the hope of salvage in quieter weather. It is almost impossible to tow a waterlogged boat under sail except dead downwind.

If you can turn over the completion of the salvage to a power boat in capable hands do not hesitate. You have done your duty.

Handling a Tender

A tender must always be loaded with crew and gear so that she floats on a level keel, whether she is to be rowed or powered by an outboard. The crew embarks one at a time, one in the stern, the next forward and so on alternately. The last to embark should be the oarsman.

In getting aboard the sailing boat disembarkation is in the reverse order.

Many accidents occur because tenders are overloaded and because crews stand up or lean out of the dinghy to grab at a moored boat.

If a heavily loaded dinghy has to be taken across waves coming from abeam it will roll wildly and may well swamp. The bow should be kept headed into the general direction of the waves and 'crabbed' across them. Very careful attention should be given to the trim of the boat and if it is even slightly overloaded, make two trips. Far better to be sure than sorry.

Tenders need to have either built-in or air-bag buoyancy and the crew should always wear lifejackets.

CHAPTER 4

SAFETY

*Personal Buoyancy – Boat Buoyancy – Fire Afloat –
Checking the Gear – Standing Rigging – Watching
the Weather – Safety in a Squall – Capsize and
Recovery – On Getting Advice*

INCREASING numbers of small boats take to the water every season. Just as regularly there is the increasing seasonal crop of accidents afloat. Most of these would not have happened if some very elementary precautions had been taken and these apply particularly to the small power boat, usually driven by an outboard engine. Roughly two-thirds of the reported mishaps affect this type of craft.

Personal Buoyancy

Some form of lifejacket should always be worn in small boats.

It takes about six pounds of buoyancy to keep an adult afloat and my own preference is for something which gives about three times this amount, does not need inflation and is always ready for use.

At least two systems have been devised to obtain buoyancy from air trapped in double-walled panels. Upon immersion the trapped air is sealed in the lifejacket and it makes no difference whether it is worn inside or outside another garment.

Of course I am aware that a press and television review came down against this type of lifejacket during 1962. The fact remains that many thousands of people use it and I have never known or heard of a failure. And whatever the boffins may recommend small-boat crews will continue to use them because of their utter simplicity.

In a small boat freedom of movement, quick movement, is

essential. If you buy a type which needs inflation bear this in mind and always see that it is partly blown up when you are in a boat. And check it for air leaks.

Boat Buoyancy

In this book I have made many references to the modern dinghy. This does not mean that older types must be ruled out. But the newcomer who has made up his mind in advance of learning to sail that he wants to own 'a good old safe clinker-built boat' will probably end up with a nail-sick craft of indifferent performance and no safety factor in the case of capsize.

The modern dinghy either has buoyancy built into watertight compartments or carries it in inflated bags fixed to the boat. The normal safety factors are impressive. One typical boat weighs 400 lb. and has buoyancy of 1,000 lb. The excess is enough to support one hundred people, let alone the three or four making up the usual complement.

An alternative to inflated buoyancy bags comes in the shape of polystyrene, a very light foam substance supplied in blocks of convenient sizes. This material has the advantage that it cannot be punctured but it needs protection from accidental damage.

If you buy a less modern type of open or half-decked boat be sure to equip it with adequate buoyancy.

Few keel boats need the incorporation of special buoyancy devices, although many more open cockpit craft such as Flying Fifteens and Swallows now carry inflated bags. The powers of a keel boat to recover from being hove down by the wind are usually sufficient, but if laid over long enough in a violent squall the hull can become waterlogged before the weight of the keel can right it.

Before putting off in a keel boat there should always be a routine check of bilges, which must be pumped dry. Propellor shaft glands, sea-cocks and lavatory outlets are all possible sources of leakage.

Very few open power craft have any form of buoyancy.

Such a craft when swamped sinks immediately because of the weight of the engine. Because they are more likely to get into the hands of the inexperienced the majority of accidents occur with this type of craft. Most of them could have been avoided by the use of additional buoyancy at a cost of a few pounds.

Fire Afloat

The obvious sources are cooking stoves and leaking fuel systems. Even an overflow of petrol into the bilges from an outboard engine tank can be dangerous. Keep a watchful eye for possible dangers and if inflammable material is kept aboard always carry an adequate number of small chemical extinguishers in a handy place. At least once a year have extinguishers checked to see that the contents are still serviceable.

Checking the Gear

Almost all the gear of a boat is subjected to strains which vary with the weight of wind and sea. It is routine for standing rigging, masts, halyards, tiller, rudder fittings and buoyancy to be checked annually. But during a season there is wear which must not go unperceived. The safety fastening of a *clevis pin*, costing twopence, may have come adrift and may lose you a mast, costing perhaps twenty pounds. Breakage or failure of gear may at the least lose you some sailing: at the most it may be dangerous.

In this hard world one usually gets what one pays for. Cheap gear is never cheap in the long run and when it comes to replacements always get the best. Never trust the sheet that will do just one more outing. Do something about it at once.

Below are listed the principal items which should be kept under constant review.

Standing Rigging

The forestay and the shrouds support the mast: if one of these fails the mast will come down, perhaps break. The consequences of this can be personal injury or a hole in the boat. The best stay material is stainless steel wire.

If there is any sign of fraying the wire must be replaced and the other points to be watched are those at the extremities where an eye is enclosed either by a splice or a metal ferrule fixed under a pressure of about one hundred tons in a special machine.

These wire stays are attached at the upper end of the mast to a fitting, preferably of stainless steel, by a clevis pin which is in turn kept in position by a safety device. This is shaped rather like a safety-pin passing through a hole in the clevis pin itself; any failure or displacement of the safety-pin can release the clevis pin and, with it, the shroud or the forestay.

Forestay and shrouds alike are kept under tension by turn-buckles at the lower ends called rigging-screws or bottle-screws. The rigging-screw itself is usually attached permanently to the stay but sometimes this is effected by means of a clevis pin passing through a fork fitting; the lower end of the rigging-screw is fixed by another clevis pin to a fitting (the *chain plate*) screwed firmly to the hull.

Every time a boat is to be taken out make a quick visual check of these vital clevis pins and their safety-pins. It is unlikely that those at the top of the mast will come adrift but at deck level they can be displaced accidentally. The chain plate must always be firmly screwed down.

Halyards come in for a great deal of wear and are under constant tension when sailing. Usually the halyard is made up of wire spliced to a rope tail for fixing to the cleat. Look for signs of wear at this splice and at the upper end where the wire passes over the sheave in the mast.

The best material for a halyard is galvanized wire with a terylene rope tail. Stainless steel wire appears to fray more quickly than galvanized. Coming increasingly into use is pre-stretched terylene rope. This is used in a continuous length without any splice to join the tail and should be considered when replacements are necessary.

Buoyancy must be checked daily. Where it is provided by

air-filled water-tight compartments the sealing round the edges of the hatches must function. Clamps which hold the hatch in position must be in working order. If the compartments are sealed by circular rubber bungs they must be in position and replaced if there are any signs of perishing.

Air bag buoyancy must be fixed firmly by webbing straps screwed to the boat. One often sees buoyancy bags tucked under thwarts and side decks without any fastening except a thin piece of codline. If the boat is capsized the bags usually float out of it.

Rudder and fittings are under constant strain. Look for the beginnings of distortion in the *hood*: this is the shaped metal piece screwed to the rudder-head into which the tiller is inserted and held by a pin.

The fittings on both the rudder and the transom must always be kept screwed home. Lose one of these and you have at once lost the use of the rudder.

The centreboard, if made of wood, may have been scored by a stone wedged between it and the casing. Stones can usually be removed by working the centreboard about but the attendant scoring is almost inevitable. At the earliest opportunity remove the centreboard, dry it out and varnish the scoring. Without protection water will attack and weaken the wood; a broken centreboard makes it impossible to sail the boat to windward.

At the bottom of the casing the centreboard is hinged to a bolt and nut. Water can leak into the boat unless the rubber washers on this hinge are screwed tightly up to the casing to effect a proper seal.

The *boom-tang* is a strip of metal fitted at the outer end of the boom so that it is free to revolve and to it is shackled a block through which runs the mainsheet. Were it not there the mainsheet would become tangled when the boom is revolved to reef the sail (see Chapter 3). Check that the screw positioning the tang is not worn or bent.

All the other gear normally carried in a sailing dinghy must be kept in a serviceable condition. The anchor and its warp must be sound and kept ready for use in an emergency. Bailer or pump must be free of leaks and, along with the indispensable plastic bucket, secured to the boat so that they will not be lost.

Keep a small bag of essential spares – shackles, clevis pins and safety-pins, a length of codline, a few tools – in a dry place in the boat. If you notice a defect whilst you are sailing, remedy it at once, even if the repair is only temporary.

Of course you cannot carry enough spares to cope with any emergency. I once saw a dinghy just before the start of a race round the Isle of Wight which carried shark-repellent powder. I think this was taking it a little too far.

Watching the Weather

In another chapter we deal with weather portents and the small-boat sailor must at all times – particularly in open water – keep a weather eye lifted. Changes and variations of wind are always written large for all to read. Intelligent anticipation and common sense remove the elements of risk.

Not a bad maxim is that there is always more wind than you think. Just as on the apparently glassy smooth day there is enough breeze to move a boat, so the brisk little wind you noticed on shore may be more than expected when you get afloat. In case of doubt, reef before sailing: it is so much easier for the novice and a reef can be quickly shaken out whilst under way if the wind moderates.

Safety in a Squall

Let us suppose that you see the signs of approaching squalls whilst you are out in a sailing boat. If you can reach a windward shore before the squall hits you this is the best course. Otherwise get the foresail down, and secure it against flapping free and reef the mainsail as quickly as possible. If your anchor warp is long enough to allow it you may prefer to ride out the squall. Except as forerunners of really heavy weather squalls are usually of short duration. If heavy weather is on the way the novice ought not to be out anyway, for prolonged stormy periods are always forecast well in advance.

If you must reef down in an emergency always tend to reduce sail by too much than too little. And reef in time: nothing can be worse than too little and too late.

The small power boat caught out in a squall should reduce speed drastically and turn into the run of the waves. The crew must seat itself so that the screw is kept beneath the surface as much as possible; if powered by an outboard engine care must be taken to see that it is not swamped. Any water breaking into the boat must be baled or pumped out immediately. If the engine is stopped by swamping the bow of the boat must be kept to the waves by rowing or paddling. Broadside on can mean rapid waterlogging and sinking.

Capsize and Recovery

At the back of the mind of all sailing novices is some apprehension of capsize. There is a mental picture of being at one moment securely sailing along and at the next of being catapulted into the water. Nothing could be farther from the facts, for a capsize is usually a comparatively gentle affair. Just as a rider is reckoned to lack experience until he falls off a horse I believe that a deliberate capsize and recovery should be part of the dinghy sailor's training. I do everything possible to encourage this in my pupils.

People often write to me about learning to sail, adding that they are strong swimmers. This has very little to do with dinghy sailing, for the first rule in a capsize is never to leave the boat. The buoyancy which is such an important factor in the modern dinghy and which can be added so easily to other boats will take care of the crew far better than an ability to swim. Assuming that personal buoyancy is worn the righting of a capsized sailing dinghy need present no difficulties.

When the boat capsizes the mast and sails lie on the surface and the vessel is on its side. This is the case even with metal masts, which are sealed at both ends so as to be buoyant. Of course if one of the crew stands or pulls on the mast it may be pulled over so that it is pointing downwards and it must be got back into the horizontal position without delay.

Capsizes naturally happen most usually in strong winds. A waterlogged boat is very unstable and if righted with sails up usually blows over again. This means that sail must come down.

In describing the rigging of a dinghy I wrote that halyards should never be turned over or knotted when secured to the cleat. Try to undo a wet knot and the force of this advice will be evident.

Having cast off the halyards from their cleats, pull down both sails. Now right the boat by having one of the crew stand on the centreboard where it projects from the bottom, pulling on the shrouds or the gunwale to help it come up. This member of the crew can get into the boat as it recovers, remembering that it will be very unstable. The remainder stay in the water, for choice holding on to the transom or bow.

As well as a bailer or a pump a plastic bucket should always be carried in sailing dinghies. Much water has to be moved and as quickly as possible, for the top of the centreboard casing will most probably be under water. This slot must be plugged as quickly as possible with anything that comes to hand. I nearly always seem to use the towelling scarf without which I never go afloat.

Bale out the dinghy until it is reasonably stable, get the crew in over the transom – entry over the side may well capsize the boat again – and you are ready to make sail. Learn something from your experience and reef down this time.

Particularly in the racing classes one often sees a boat righted without getting sails down. The crews are usually experienced and by teamwork manage something that may be beyond the powers of a novice. Try it once, if you like, but if your first righting is followed by another capsize, get the sails down.

Whatever happens, stay with the boat. It may be that halyards will not run free or other difficulties hinder your recovery. In or near any sailing centre it is almost impossible for a capsize to go unobserved. Somebody will do something to help.

In your early days of sailing avoid the boisterous days when the wind may be too much for you. Whilst it is true that help is nearly always available a capsize caused by your inexperience can put others to a great deal of trouble and a risk of damage to your rescuers' boat.

On a quiet day try a deliberate capsize and recovery. Have a friend stand by in another boat if you like. Once you have done it and recovered, capsizing should have lost its terrors.

On Getting Advice

Nothing is so infuriating as the novice who asks a fellow member of his club if there is too much wind for him, is told that there probably is, and who then announces that he'll risk it and go out. Usually this ends by somebody else having to spend time and effort in helping with a rescue. Not infrequently the new owner or his crew is frightened off sailing for life.

The culprit is usually one who has been penned up in an office during the week. That sail at the weekend has never been far from his thoughts and having driven sixty miles to get it, nothing will put him off. Ignoring the fact that others who are sailing have more experience, he asks advice and at once rejects it.

It may be that an excursion to a particular place has been planned. The combination of winds and tides may make another destination a simpler goal. Ask somebody who knows and accept the advice. Try to find another boat bound for the same destination and sail in company.

John Seymour writes: 'I am inclined to err on the side of going rather than not going, and this is about the worst fault you can have in a mariner.'

Sound advice can always be had: but it will not be offered.

CHAPTER 5

WEATHER AND TIDES

*Weather Reporting System – Wind Strengths –
Reading the Sky – The Tides – Tidal Streams*

IF you meet an acquaintance in the street the odds are that you will exchange a remark about the weather. In sailing centres it is the number one topic, affecting the plans of all.

Clubs arranging racing courses will do so with a time limit in mind and the contestants will have to decide whether to rig their mainsails 'hard' or 'soft'. Many dinghy helmsmen have alternative crews for light and heavy wind conditions, and last summer I even saw one devoted crew walk into the water up to her shoulders wearing three sweaters to soak up an extra weight of water. Any racing course in tidal waters will inevitably pass through waters where the wind will be knocking up a chop when it blows against the tide, and tactics must be considered in advance.

The family sailing off for a picnic must also make plans. Will the wind be blowing onshore at the destination? If so, would it not be better to go somewhere else? What will the tide be doing? At what time should the return be made so as to get on the mooring or haul up in comfort? Will the wind hold? Or strengthen? Or die away in the evening?

Local knowledge can help to answer many of these questions, for the general weather forecasts cover a wide area and local variations follow a pattern which you will discern in time. Fishermen who swallowed the anchor years ago will say, for example, that the wind will come up with the tide. It is difficult to work out any physical reason for this but it is so in nine cases out of ten. At the spring and autumn equinoxes the tides are at their highest: so, all too often, are the winds.

Rain before seven often *does* mean fine before eleven. The old saw 'Red in the morning, shepherds' warning' has its origin in the Bible. A halo round the moon *does* nearly always mean that the next day will be rainy, and 'Mackerel sky and mares' tails make tall ships carry low sails'.

Weather Reporting System

In a country which has no climate – only weather – nearly everybody can read a meteorological chart with some degree of understanding. They are published in most newspapers and appear on the television screens. And by the way, don't blackguard the B B C for the weather forecasts; it only transmits the Meteorological Office predictions.

As a sailing man you will be affected by the general forecast for the area, modified by the strictly local quirks which knowledge and observation will help you to master. Some understanding of the origins of the winds and the weather they bring may help to bring the subject to life.

Meteorological charts are the situation maps in a vast and endless struggle between huge main air masses covering anything from a half-million square miles upwards. Within these masses are potentials of destruction as great or greater than any hydrogen bomb. Fortunately for Britain and Europe in general our weather maps show only the local skirmishes in the ceaseless war. The main battles for the ascendancy of one air mass over another are usually fought far from our shores and leave behind hurricane and tidal wave destruction.

In the northern hemisphere the main air masses which affect our weather come from either the Arctic and Polar Continental area, Maritime Polar area (the west coast of North America), Continental Maritime area (North Africa and southern Europe) or the Maritime Tropical area (the southern part of the North Atlantic). The first brings cold air, usually sunny and dry: the second brings fair weather and a possibility of thunderstorms: the third brings winter storms from the south: the fourth brings settled weather of the best kind in summer.

Any of these air masses can pick up other characteristics as they move and a large amount of the background of forecasting is the tracking and identification of the origin of each. The collisions of the air masses, sometimes much modified by the areas over which they have travelled, but still retaining their basic characteristics, is the origin of cold and warm fronts which so much affect the weather. Movement of the main air masses derives from the rotation of the earth about the axis. Winds are shaped by the movement of an air mass from a high pressure area (where the weather is usually fine) into a lower pressure rain area. Of course this does not mean that there is no wind in fine weather but the transition from rain to fine usually has a windy period.

Let us have a look at the terms commonly used in weather reports.

Isobars are lines joining points of equal barometric pressure based on reports fed in from ground stations, weather ships or aircraft in flight. The isobars plot the valleys of depression and the peaks of high pressure exactly like the contour lines on land maps.

The barometric pressures are recorded in millibars, one of which is equivalent to the pressure of a layer of water 1 centimetre in depth.

Fronts mark the line of collision between air masses of different origins and characteristics. It might be supposed that they would tend to mix but this is not so. If a warm air mass gains supremacy a warm front forms : a cold front builds up when a cold air mass prevails. The path of the warm front is marked by light rain increasing in intensity until the front passes : the cold front is preceded by showers and thunderstorms in the summer and by sleet or snow in the winter.

Troughs of low pressure begin to form when some local influence dents a stationary front and a depression then builds up rapidly. The front divides itself into cold and warm sections : when the cold front begins to overtake the warm front an occlusion is formed and a depression is centred at the junction of the two types of front. Eventually the depression

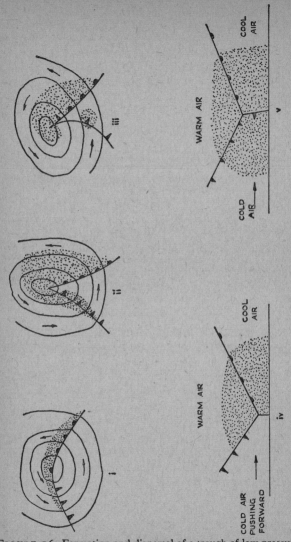

FIGURE 16 Formation and dispersal of a trough of low pressure

fills, rain ceases to fall and more settled weather returns.

The prevailing winds in Britain blow from a westerly direction and two situations are used as the basis of forecasting: these are those in the Atlantic and the general European continental areas. Figure 17 plots a typical Atlantic situation on

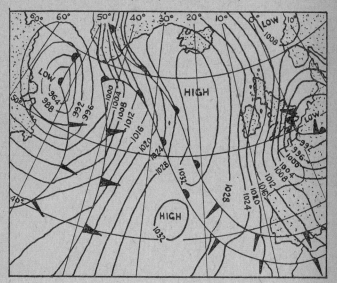

FIGURE 17 Atlantic weather map

a given day and Figure 18 shows the situation forecast for the day following. Much can and does happen to upset the predicted weather and the difference between the two maps is that the first is an actual situation and the second a forecast only.

The Atlantic map shows a low-pressure area off Newfoundland from the centre of which runs a short warm front and a much longer cold front. The latter may occlude and deepen the depression or it may later straighten up and eliminate the bad weather. In any case the result will not be felt in Britain for some days, if at all.

In mid Atlantic a cold front is rapidly overtaking a warm front and a trough is forming, falling away from the 1032

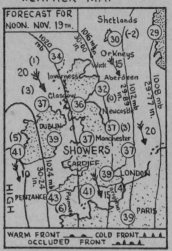

ISSUED AT 6-30 p.m.

BLACK CIRCLES SHOW IN FAHRENHEIT TEMPERATURES EXPECTED: THE EQUIVALENT TEMPERATURE IN CENTIGRADE IS GIVEN ALONGSIDE IN BRACKETS. ARROWS INDICATE WIND DIRECTION AND SPEED IN M.P.H. PRESSURE IN MILLIBARS AND INCHES.

FIGURE 18 British Isles forecast map

high-pressure area north of the Azores. Parallel to the eastern leg of the occluded mid-Atlantic trough runs another front, warm at the northern end and cold at the southern end. These two frontal systems may merge, kink in the middle and thrust a trough towards Britain from the south-west. Certainly they will have an effect upon the forecast for the following day.

Figure 18 is the forecast for the day following. North-westerly winds have moved the high-pressure centre down from a position south of Ireland to the south-west of Ireland and the winds circulating about it blow coldly from the north. In this instance the forecasters were right but the overall situation was complex enough for them to be wrong. The two low-pressure areas to the north and east could have joined together to alter the whole pattern of weather, and it is these unpredictable variations which make weather forecasting the thankless task it is.

Wind Strengths

The small-boat sailor depends on the wind to move his craft and to bring his weather. In the northern hemisphere it blows anti-clockwise round the low-pressure foul-weather systems and in the reverse direction round the fair-weather highs. This means that, as a low advances with increasing wind strengths near the centre, the wind will tend to back in an anti-clockwise direction. When it veers in a clockwise direction this is an indication that the low-pressure area is filling up.

It will be useful to you to know where bad weather is lying. If you face the wind it will be upon your right hand and this discovery by a Dutch professor gives it the name of Buys Ballot's Rule. In the southern hemisphere the low pressure area lies on the left hand.

Wind speeds are often measured by a scale drawn up by Admiral Sir Francis Beaufort in the nineteenth century and it lingers on with us like rods, poles and perches. It is invariably used in radio shipping forecasts but other sources about which I shall be writing later give the wind speed in knots.

The speeds quoted in the Beaufort Scale are for observation on land and a good maxim for the small-boat sailor is, 'There's always more wind than you think'. In your early days Force 4 should be your upper limit and if more than this is forecast either don't go out or stay near your base. If you are

BEAUFORT SCALE OF WIND FORCE

Beaufort Number	Description of Wind	Speed in m.p.h.	Effects on Land
0	Calm	Less than 1	Smoke rises vertically.
1	Light airs	1–3	Smoke shows direction; usually insufficient to move weather vanes.
2	Light breeze	4–6	Weather vanes move; wind felt on face.
3	Gentle breeze	7–10	Wind moves flags; twigs in constant movement.
4	Moderate breeze	11–16	Dust is raised and small branches are in movement.
5	Fresh breeze	17–21	Small trees sway.
6	Strong breeze	22–27	Large branches move.
7	Moderate gale	28–33	Larger trees sway; walking against the wind is not easy.
8	Fresh gale	34–40	Twigs break from trees; walking against the wind is difficult.
9	Strong gale	41–47	Slates and chimney pots blown away from roofs.
10	Whole gale	48–55	Buildings damaged and trees uprooted.
11	Storm	56–63	Widespread general damage.
12	Hurricane	64–71	Devastation on a wide scale.

FIGURE 19

attempting to make an estimate of a Beaufort Force you must make your observations in an area clear of obstruction. To try to do so in a walled garden is useless.

A useful device can be found in the chandlery stores which reads off the wind speed on a scale when a shaped funnel is pointed into the wind. Here again the reading must be taken clear of shelter: if you get one of these instruments and have young children, hide it. The temptation to blow down it is overwhelming and it then ceases to work.

If you can read a meteorological map and suffer from television you have at least two opportunities during an evening of seeing a forecast for the following day. The B B C issues shipping forecasts on the long wave Light Programme at weekday clock times of 06.45, 13.40 17.58 and 24.02: the second forecast is at 11.55 on Sundays.

Some short wave navigational direction finders are capable of picking up weather information on the Trawler band at more frequent intervals.

From May until October the B B C includes a holiday weather forecast on both Light Programme frequencies at 8.55 am and this always includes wind information for sailing purposes.

In the front portion of all telephone directories you will find numbers to ring for local information and perhaps these are the most valuable sources of all. The broadcast predictions are necessarily based on information some hours old in order to make up a general picture. The local sources have more recent information about regional situations; some of these will be Naval or Royal Air Force stations and you must make it clear that you are inquiring about surface winds, or you will otherwise find yourself getting much puzzling information about winds at 30,000 ft.

Reading the Sky

You cannot have too many sources of weather information and you should train yourself to watch the differing colours of the sky and the shape and movement of clouds. All these are portents of what may be expected in the next few hours, sometimes for the next day.

A yellowish sky is a forerunner of heavy wind and rain, especially towards the end of the day. The blow may not materialize on the following day but come it certainly will within forty-eight hours.

You may very well go wrong in assessing the meaning of a red sky, for whilst a red morning glow in the east is a bad sign the converse is not always true. An even glow to the west at sunset is the forerunner of good weather but if it is reflected by clouds across the sky towards the east be sure that heavy winds are on the way.

A soft blue sky is associated with settled weather and a darker blue is the sign of increasing winds and a change in direction of the wind.

These differing colours are closely related to the amounts of moisture in the atmosphere and many of the old saws relating to the weather are bound up with them.

There are three main types of cloud and sometimes they combine to form sub divisions.

The highest cloud formation is cirrus and, always found at great height, it may extend to the stratosphere. Cirrus often takes the form usually known as 'mares' tails' and when these are criss-crossed in the sky a weather change is on the way. If at a lower altitude it looks like a shoal of fish, rain is coming within twelve hours.

If the mares' tails point upwards at the narrow end rain is coming: if they point downwards you may expect fine and dry weather.

Probably the most familiar cloud is the cumulus and in differing shapes it brings either dry or wet weather. In the summer it moves across the sky in soft white banks and usually disperses at sunset. Where it erupts from the main mass in towering grey shapes showers may be expected, usually local and lasting only for a short period. If cumulus builds up towards the end of the day prolonged rain is probable.

All too familiar is the stratus cloud stretched across the sky in a grey sheet, often without a break. Sometimes only a few hundred feet above the ground, any thickening of the sheet round high ground foretells probable rain. Stratus is more susceptible to dispersal by local influences than the other types of cloud and it is sometimes difficult to believe when sailing in bright sunshine that only an hour before the sky overhead was hidden by an unbroken sheet of grey cloud. Once the sun penetrates stratus in sufficient strength it begins to warm the land, the air over it rises and a fine breeze comes in from the sea to sweep away the remnants of cloud. From this comes the saw about 'enough blue sky to patch a sailor's breeches'.

All the changing picture of the sky has meaning.

Small clouds which shrink and disappear towards evening foretell good weather on the morrow. If they build up to cover most of the sky you must expect a change to unsettled conditions. When the edges of summer clouds merge softly into a pale blue sky fine weather will continue. If they stand out sharply against a sky of darker blue, look out for a blow.

A slow and even movement of cloud across the sky foretells good weather just as swift movement predicts more wind later on. Where clouds at different levels move in different directions the wind will soon shift to the line taken by the higher cloud.

When cloud moves from an easterly to a westerly direction it will usually be dry but if rain comes with it you must be prepared for a long spell.

Towards the end of a spell of good weather very high clouds begin to form as the signs of a change. The longer the time taken for the change to come, the more prolonged is the bad weather period.

The Tides

As the moon moves round the earth it exerts a magnetic pull on the great water masses and so causes the tides. This pull is strongest when the moon is nearest the earth at a period in the lunar month and it is then that tides are at their highest spring levels. Associated with the high springs are very low ebb tides, just as the lower neap tides between spring periods bring with them more water at the bottom of the ebb.

Tidal heights and times are a matter of prediction by hydrographers and are based on the assumption of a complete absence of wind. Gales will force the water mass to follow their direction and will either increase or decrease the predicted height, sometimes by many feet, and accelerate or retard the time of a predicted high tide. In recent years gales at spring tide periods have brought disasters to the West Country and Holland and a close watch is kept upon weather trends on the vulnerable coasts.

The small-boat sailor is affected to a lesser degree but must always be aware of what is to be expected.

Very approximately, for local coastal formation and tidal currents have much influence, tides make up for about seven and a quarter hours on the flood and run out on the ebb for about five and a quarter hours. Again very approximately, this means that high tide is about one hour later each day. One thing is very clear: the ebb runs for a shorter period than the flood and it follows that if the same amount of water runs out faster than it flows in, the ebb will have a stronger current than the flood.

If you make proper use of a tide table (and you *must* have one) it will not be long before you begin to plan sailing in relation to the tides. Nothing is more sure than that time and tide wait for no man: probably you will learn this the hard way by leaving it too late and having to tack back to your base with the wind and a strong ebb against you.

On spring tides you must also remember to give your boat the full scope of the mooring chain. If it is shortened up too much the extra rise in water level and the buoyancy of your boat between them may pull your mooring out of the ground. Or the mooring may hold and pull the bow of your boat beneath the level of the rising tide.

You will find that local tide tables are available in all sailing centres and that they usually cover several places in the same locality. Times of high tides will vary between each place and a list will show the number of minutes to be added or subtracted to give a true prediction for each, subject always to the strength and direction of the wind.

Local tables are usually laid out in eight columns giving:
1. The day of the week
2. The date
3. The type of tide, i.e. Spring or Neap
4. Moon phase – First Quarter, Full, Last Quarter and New Moon
5. Time of morning tide
6. Height of morning tide
7. Time of afternoon tide
8. Height of afternoon tide.

Ten columns are occasionally made so as to include the times of low tides.

Column 3 will have marked in it an elongated 'N' (neaps) or a large 'S' (springs) and there are two of each in each lunar period. Taking as an example the month of October 1962, at Portsmouth, the lowest neap tide is at 10′ 4″ for 06.42 on the 8th, the moon then being a little past the first quarter. From then on each tide shows an increase until at 12.37 on the 14th it rises to 14′ 9″. In column 4 on the 12th appears the letter 'P' indicating that on that date the moon is at the position of perigee in orbit, the point when it is nearest to the earth and exerting the maximum pull. In column 3 an elongated 'S' marks the spring tide period and from the afternoon tide of the 12th until the morning tide of the 17th the heights are in italics to show their association with abnormal lows.

The tides then begin to cut in height until at 20.07 on the 22nd they are down to 10′ 3″ after which they begin to build up again to the second period of springs, culminating in 13′ 4″ at 11.45 on the 29th. On the 26th column 4 shows the letter 'A' to indicate the apogee, the period in orbit when the moon is farthest from the earth. The new moon of the 28th, now in line with the sun, has already begun to exert a pull on the tides, but not so powerfully as at the perigee. Consequently none of the low tides will be abnormally below the usual level.

Tidal Streams

In the normal creek or estuary upon which you will find most sailing centres there is nothing very complicated in the tidal streams. Tides flow in and ebb out again, and except for occasional eddies which may help the racing helmsman who knows his water, the pattern is quite straightforward.

Outside the creeks and estuaries coastal and underwater configurations will have much influence on the direction and speed of tidal streams. These may sometimes be found at some distance from the feature which originates them and minor but still powerful streams crossing even more powerful streams will set up an awkward race. Typical of these are the races off Portland and St Catherine's Point on the Isle of Wight, both induced by features fairly distant from their incidence.

Tidal streams are indicated on charts and tables and show their estimated speed and direction at differing states of the tide.

The subject is more fully dealt with in Chapter 6.

The LEADER, a multi-purpose sailing dinghy of high performance which is suitable for the newcomer

The WAYFARER, a sturdy
16 ft. high performance
dinghy which also makes
a good family boat

The ZENITH,
crew watching warily
as the spinnaker
pulls them downwind

The TRICORN, a popular
first boat which combines
the sailing qualities of a
class dinghy with two-berth
accommodation

The ALBACORE, a 15 ft.
racing dinghy which is
also a very suitable
family boat

The MIRROR dinghy, which has grown very rapidly in numbers over a short perio[d]

The SHEARWATER catamaran, one of the most successful multi-hull designs

The CADET, a classic racing ding[hy] for juniors up to sixteen years of a[ge]

CHAPTER 6

BUOYAGE AND NAVIGATION

*Buoyage Systems–Navigation and Pilotage–Rules of
the Road – Planning a Passage – Executing the Plan*

AT some stage in your sailing career you will no doubt hope
to go cruising in a keel boat farther afield than the creeks
or estuaries in which I hope you will have started. Perhaps
your imagination has presented you with a slightly roman-
ticized picture of yourself standing on a heaving deck taking
sights with a sextant, coupled with the uneasy thought that
you have not the faintest idea how the thing works or even
what it is supposed to do.

Be easy in your mind, for this complex instrument will only
come your way when you have qualified for the long voyages
when you will be out of sight of land for many days, perhaps
weeks. Deep sea navigation is a subject in itself and if you
feel you must learn about it in anticipation of that distant day
when you start on a world cruise, you cannot do better if you
live near London than to join the Little Ship Club and enrol
on a course. If you live elsewhere you may learn very well by
taking a correspondence course such as that conducted by
Captain O. M. Watts.

Coastal navigation presents less complex problems and
will be quite enough for you to be going on with. The buoyage
systems are the signposts of the sea and accurate coastal navigation takes you by dead reckoning from one set of signposts
to those at your planned destination. To achieve this you
must know the speed of your ship through the water and over
the ground – not necessarily the same thing – and to know
your exact position at all times. You must also have means
of knowing the direction in which to steer and to determine
the depth of the water below your keel.

Buoyage Systems

Too many owners and charterers of small cruising boats go to sea without any knowledge of the significance of navigational buoys. Most of them may be for the guidance of larger vessels than your own but until you know the channel, stick to the buoys or other marks' which define it. In your local waters you will soon learn what latitude you can give yourself but take no chances in new anchorages.

Buoys fall into four categories, those left to starboard or port when going with the main flood stream, middle ground buoys at the junction of channels, and wreck buoys. To each of these except wreck buoys topmarks may be added and many carry a lighting system having definite characteristics to help in identification at night. Others carry a bell, sometimes operated by the movement of the sea to give warning in fog, sometimes mechanically at specified intervals. Figure 20 illustrates the Trinity House Buoyage System.

Starboard-hand Buoys

Colour	Black or black-and-white chequered, marked B. or B.W.Cheq. on the chart
Shape	Conical
Topmark (if any)	Black triangle
Light (if any)	1, 3 or 5 white flashes

Port-hand Buoys

Colour	Red or red and white chequered, marked R. or R.W.Cheq. on the chart
Shape	Can
Topmark (if any)	Red square
Light (if any)	1, 2, 3 or 4 red flashes, alternatively 2, 4 or 6 white flashes

Middle-Ground Buoys

Colour	Red and white horizontal bands to indicate a main channel to the right or channels of equal importance, marked on charts as R.W.H.B.

	Black and white horizontal bands to indicate a main channel to the left, B.W.H.B. on the chart
Shape	Spherical
Topmarks (if any)	Where the main channel is on the right, a red can to mark the outer and a red 'T' to mark the inner end
	Where the main channel is on the left, a black triangle or cone to mark the outer end and a black diamond to mark the inner end
Lights	White or red

Wreck Buoys

Colour	Green, frequently carrying the word 'Wreck' in white
Shape	Conical
Light (if any)	Flashing green

Wreck buoys are usually laid on the deeper water side of the obstruction.

The majority of buoys are lettered with a name corresponding to that on the chart to aid positive identification. Charts also quote the light characteristics of buoys which display them.

A flashing light is one in which the dark periods are longer than the light periods or where the periods are equal in duration. (Fl. 3 sec. means 3 seconds of darkness followed by a 1 second flash.)

An occulting light is one in which the light periods are longer than the dark periods. (Occ. red ev. 10 secs. means one which goes out for a second every 10 seconds.)

A group flashing light is one which flashes two or three times, repeating the pattern after a specified number of seconds. Gp. Fl. (4) ev. 15 secs. means a group of 4 white flashes of 1 second each every 15 seconds.)

Example of the lighted buoy characteristics as marked on a chart are enclosed in brackets after each definition quoted above. So as to avoid complication Trinity House has adopted

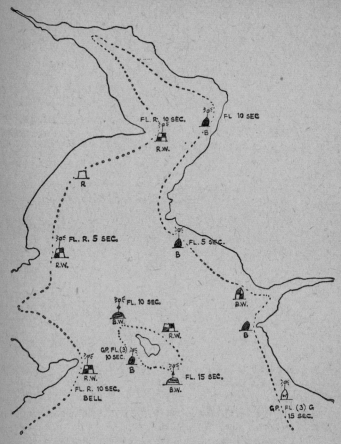

FL. R. 10 SEC.

FL 10 SEC.

R.W.

B

R

FL. R. 5 SEC.

FL. 5 SEC.

R.W.

B

FL. 10 SEC.

B.W.

B.W.

R.W.

B

GP. FL. (3)
10 SEC.

B

FL. 15 SEC.

R.W.

B.W.

FL. R. 10 SEC.
BELL

GP. FL. (3) G
15 SEC.

FIGURE 20 Trinity House Buoyage System

lighting mechanisms which are limited in number, but the buoyage layout in a particular area is completely distinctive.

In some cases beacons on poles display buoy symbols and/or lights which follow the general system. This is usually in shoal water or at the entrances to harbours.

Navigational and racing buoys must not be confused and failure to distinguish between them may put you aground. Clubs lay buoys, usually black and white barrels floating on their sides, sometimes displaying a flag topmark, to mark racing courses. Occasionally you will find a non-standard topmark of the same type on a navigational buoy, but this concession by Trinity House is never allowed to confuse navigators in main shipping channels.

Navigation and Pilotage

Here are the basic requirements for coastal navigation:

1. An accurate compass: an additional hand-bearing compass is also useful.
2. Charts to cover your cruising ground.
3. A set of navigational instruments – pencil, rubber, protractor, dividers and a parallel rule.
4. Tide tables appropriate to the area or a current Read's Almanac.
5. A patent log to ascertain speed through the water.
6. A leadline or echo sounder.

If a radio direction finder can be afforded this will reduce many of your problems since it fixes your position at all times with complete accuracy.

I wrote earlier that deep sea navigation will not concern you in the early days. If you are wise you will start with daylight passages from one port to another. Dead reckoning navigation between them and the pilotage problems of moving into an anchorage you have never seen before will exercise your common sense and skill.

The first requirement is an accurate compass and it should

preferably be as large as is convenient. Nothing is more difficult than to steer a course by a minute instrument about the size of the average wristwatch, and accuracy is much greater with a larger bowl.

The parts of a compass are simple.

A needle swings freely on a pivot within the bowl, into which is sealed a liquid to damp violent oscillation. To the needle is attached a compass card marked off with the cardinal points and degrees from 0° to 360° to complete the radius of a full circle.

Now you may have heard of an exercise called 'Boxing the Compass'. This consists of taking the four cardinal points of North, East, South and West and subdividing them into the inter-cardinals of North-East, South-East and so on. Further subdivisions and subdivisions of subdivisions eventually produce near-incomprehensibles such as East-North-East or North-East by East.

The parrot repetition of these points in sequence right round the compass used to be reckoned as the basis of sound navigation training. Perhaps it still is in some quarters.

If you buy a vessel fitted with a genuinely antique compass, scrap it and get something more modern. You will save on aspirins in the long run. The modern compass lays more emphasis on degrees and you will find it much easier to think of East as 90°, South as 180° and so on.

You will know that the compass needle points to the magnetic north and this has nothing to do with the true or geographical north upon which is based the drawing of charts and maps. The magnetic north pole further complicates the situation by moving about from year to year, fortunately on a predictable path. This divergence of the magnetic from the true north is known as the variation of the compass. Being relatively small, failure to adjust calculations accordingly would make little difference in a short passage but could put you miles out in a longer voyage.

If you spread out a chart you will find compass roses upon it at several points. These are two concentric circles, of which the outer gives true bearings and the inner the magnetic. The year of issue is also printed on the chart together with the annual variation, from which may be calculated the correction to be applied. But let us go back to the compass itself.

Not only is the needle pointed to the north by magnetic attraction: it is also influenced by metal parts of the vessel, ballast, engine, anchors and chain and the resultant error is called deviation. Most of this error can be countered by the insertion of small magnets in a part of the compass whilst the yacht is swung on a mooring through known bearings. This is not a job for a beginner and should be carried out by a compass adjuster if you think it necessary. If you are buying a new yacht it should have been done before delivery and unless any major change has taken place in the magnetic components of an older boat the original deviation table will serve.

This table is drawn up after the correcting magnets have been inserted: these will not eliminate deviation on all points of the compass but will give you the small corrections which must be applied to perhaps fourteen of the sixteen check bearings taken by the adjuster.

The practical applications of these two variants are explained later.

I listed a hand-bearing compass as a useful piece of equipment. It is used in taking one, two or more quick visual bearings on known points to give a 'fix' of position. Nothing is embodied to correct deviation, for the check is only a rough one. I saw recently a letter in the yachting press which related an experience of marked deviation in a hand-bearing compass caused by metal in spectacles. This had never occurred to me previously and is clearly something to be remembered.

All charts are based upon those prepared by the Admiralty hydrographers. Surveys are constantly being carried out, particularly in the narrow waters leading to the major ports. Corrections which should be made to charts are detailed in Admiralty Notices to Mariners and when buying it is as well to deal with a specializing chart agent or a reputable chandler.

Marked upon the chart should be the last date to which it is corrected, and since many shoals shift under the influence of gales an alteration in the position of buoys may have taken place.

You will not want to read through the Notices to Mariners, for much of the matter will not affect you. Most clubs post those relating to their area and the yachting press summarizes those of interest to yachtsmen. These often draw attention to the moving of the less important coastwise buoys for maintenance during the winter and their replacement in the spring. Charts may always be taken to one of the recognized agents for correction.

Based on the Admiralty charts are some excellent tinted versions which clearly mark shoal areas as well as showing soundings in necessarily small figures. Those prepared by Stanfords and by Imray and Wilson are good examples.

All charts fall into one of three main categories.

Passage charts are on a small scale, show the principal features and are used for plotting the main course between leaving one anchorage and entering another.

Coastal charts show inshore hazards on a larger scale.

Harbour plans are on a still larger scale and depict every detail of an approach to an anchorage. Within it are shown good holding ground for anchoring, the location of shipyards and slips, hards for landing from dinghies, fresh water points and even post offices.

A most useful addition for those cruising in the South is Adlard Coles' *Pocket Pilot for the South Coast*. This shows in a standard pattern aerial and surface photographs of the ports and harbourages, the leading marks into them, a clear harbour plan and concise textual sailing directions. All this is available in other publications but the convenient size of the *Pocket Pilot* strongly commends it.

A mass of information is given on all charts and the first thing you should ascertain is whether the soundings are given in feet or fathoms: the latter is six feet, by the way. Soundings are measured from a datum line taken as the average of low water at spring tides. At certain periods of exceptionally high springs these may be below the datum and to emphasize this tide tables quote the relevant tidal heights in italics.

On the Admiralty charts some soundings are underlined to show that they stand by that amount above water level at low tide. The tinted and coloured charts emphasize this and also embody the underlined figures. If the unit used is the fathom, depths or heights less than this are shown in feet (o4). Nearer the shores where anchoring might be planned the type of bottom is shown in abbreviated form and the nature of some of these will show at once whether an anchor might hold. Other areas or invisible submarine cables are marked as being prohibited anchorages.

Against each buoy is marked the distinguishing characteristics and the name painted upon it. Take, for example, a buoy in the Solent marked 'Fl. 3 sec., Bell 30 secs., Calshot'; underneath the letter 'B' shows it to be black and therefore to be left to starboard approaching from the seaward, lighted for 1 second between each dark period of 3 seconds and having a bell which sounds every 30 seconds. (A word of warning here: when you later venture to the coast of France you must remember that 'B' will not stand for 'black' but for 'blanc' – white.) A conventional sign of a very obvious shipwreck is marked against the appropriate buoys and others having no connexion with navigation – measured mile buoys, for instance – are shown and identified.

On one corner of the chart will be a detail of the tidal streams and these are to be important to you when you come to lay off a course. Enclosed in a diamond are various letters corresponding to others on the chart showing the strengths and directions of the tidal streams at various times, related to high tides at a port of reference.

Turning to the shore little detail is shown, as might be expected. Coastwise roads and railways where traffic might be seen, prominent landmarks, conspicuous spires and water-towers are all there to help in positive identification. From nearly every harbour runs out a dotted line and an abbre-

FIGURE 21

BRITISH CHART ABBREVIATIONS

Nature of the Bottom			
b. ....blue	ab^t .....about	I, I^t .....Island, Islet	Occas ..Occasional
blk....black	Alt. ....alternating	in. ....Inches	Ord ....Ordinary
br. ...brown	Anch^e ...Anchorage	irreg. ....irregular	Pass ...Passage
brk. ...broken	B. .....Bay, Black	kn. ......knot	Pen^{la} ..Peninsula
c. ....coarse	B^k ....Bank	L.B. .....Life Boat	P^k .....Peak
chk. ..chalk	B^n ....Beacon	L^{dg} ..... Leading (Lights or Beacons) Landing (Place)	Pos^n, P ..Position
cl, Cy. .clay	Br.......Bridge	L^e .....Ledge	Prom^y ..Promontory
d. ....dark	Cas .....Castle	L^r .....Lower	Prov^l ...Provisional
f. ....fine	C.G. ....Coast Guard	L.S.S. ....Life Saving Station	R......River, Red
g, G. ...gravel	Ch. .....Church or Chapel	L^t .....Light	Rem^{ble} ..Remarkable
gn. ...green	Chan. ...Channel	L^{t}H^o ....Lighthouse	R^l ......Reef
gy. ...gray	Cheq. ...Chequered	L^{t}F......Fixed	R^k ......Rock
h. ....hard	Ch^y .....Chimney	L^{t}Fl. .....Flashing	R.S. ....Rocket Station
l. ....large	Conspic. .Conspicuous	L^{t}Gp.Fl. ..Group Flashing	Ru. ....Ruin
lt. ...light	Cov.....Covers, Covered	L^{t}Gp.Occ..Group Occulting	R^y .....Railway
m, M. .mud	Cr.......Creek	L^{t}Occ. ...Occulting	s. ......seconds
oys. ...oysters	D. ......Doubtful	L^{t}Rev. ...Revolving	S^d .....Sound
oz. ....ooze	dist. ....distant		Sem. ....Semaphore
	Dr., dr. ..Dries		Sh. ....Shoal
			Sig. ....Signal

peb, P. pebbles	Estab ...Establishment	L^t.Ves .....Light Vessel	Sp, Spr. Spring Tides
r, R. ..rock	ev. ......every	L.W. .....Low Water	St^n .....Station
rd. ....red	fl. ......flash	m. ....miles, minutes	Str. ....Strait
s. .....sand	Fl. ......Flood	Mag. ......Magnetic	Tel. ....Telegraph
sft. ....soft	F^m, f^{ms} ..Fathom, fathoms	Mag^z ..Magazine	T^r .....Tower
sh. ....shells	F.S. .....Flagstaff	M.H.W.S...Mean High Water	(U).....Unwatched
shin. ..shingle	f^t. ......foot or feet	Springs	Uncov. ..Uncovers,
sm. ...small	G. ......Gulf	M.L.W.S...Mean Low Water	Uncovered
st. ....stones	G., G^n ...Green	Springs	Var^n ....Variation
stf. ....stiff	Gp. ......Group	Mid. ......Middle	Vel. ....Velocity
w. ....white	h, hrs. ..hour, hours	min. ......minutes	vert^l ....vertical
wd. ...weed	H^d ......Head	Mon^t ......Monument	Vil. ....Village
y. .....yellow	H^n ......Haven	M^t ......Mountain	vis. ....visible
	Ho. ......House	Mth ......Mouth	V.S. ....Vertical Stripes
	H^r ......Harbour, Higher	N^o ......Number	W., Wh. White
	hor ......horizontal	Np. ......Neap Tide	Wh^f ....Wharf
	H.S. .....Horizontal	obsc^d ...obscured	Y......Yellow
	Stripes	Obs^y......Observatory	Y^{ds} .....Yards
	H.W. ....High Water		

viated description of two leading marks to be kept in line and so guide vessels to the entrance buoys.

Above is a detail of abbreviations found on British charts.

For working on the charts you will need dividers for measuring off distance, a parallel rule for laying off bearings from a compass rose, a hexagonal H.B. pencil and a soft rubber. In case you wonder why a hexagonal pencil is specified this is simply to prevent it rolling off the chart table with the movement of your vessel in a seaway.

Area tide tables or *Read's Almanac* must not be forgotten. The latter publication gives a mass of information on every possible problem you are likely to meet, but see that it is for the current year.

The distance run through the water must be read from a patent log and the most widely used is Walker's. This is operated by a small propellor towed astern on the end of a long line, which is itself rotated by the propellor and gives a distance run figure on a glass-faced dial. The patent log is brought into use when you are clear of your point of departure and the line must be hauled inboard as the destination is approached.

Coming into increasing use are other recording logs which also give speed through the water at any time rather like a car speedometer. These are operated by a forward-facing pipe well below water level and when first introduced were said to be unreliable because the pipe could be blocked by seaweed, or by mud if the vessel takes the ground. The troubles now seem to have been eliminated by various means.

When in shoal water you will need to know the depth below your keel: the most usual method of sounding is by using a leadline, a sinker attached to a light rope which is marked off at intervals. A full-size hand leadline is about 25 fathoms in length, marked off (from the sinker end) as follows:

2 fathoms – 2 pieces of leather
3 fathoms – 3 pieces of leather
5 fathoms – White cloth

7 fathoms – Red cloth
10 fathoms – Leather with hole
13 fathoms – Blue cloth
15 fathoms – White cloth
17 fathoms – Red cloth
20 fathoms – Short lanyard knotted twice

The differing materials and shapes, notably the first three, help in taking soundings in darkness.

It is unlikely that you will be interested in taking soundings of more than 5 fathom depths and a leadline of about 6 fathoms overall should be quite enough. Many yachtsmen use their own private markings, and this is perfectly satisfactory so long as everyone aboard knows their meanings.

Echo sounders are now coming into more general use and are reasonable in cost. They are extremely accurate and always ready for use at the flick of a switch. Instal one if you can afford it.

Another piece of equipment which should be bought if the budget will allow it is a radio direction-finder. In the earlier patterns these instruments occupied a good deal of valuable space but the introduction of transistor valves and smaller direction-finding loops has brought down the size. You will need a radio receiver in any case, and for a relatively small extra cost you can have all the advantages of modern aids to navigation. The yacht radio direction-finders all incorporate receivers covering all frequencies, and the 'trawler band' with its frequent weather reports cannot usually be brought in on small portable radios.

Using fixed beacons at known positions ashore, R.D.F. gives bearings on any three which are convenient. The three bearing lines traced on a chart show the exact position of your vessel at any time and you will most value your instrument in thick weather.

Rules of the Road

All traffic systems must be governed by a set of rules and those applying to the sea are very full and detailed. Basically they apply as much to boats sailing on a gravel pit as to ocean liners. Six basics should be memorized:

1. When running free you must give way to a boat which is close hauled.
2. If you are on port tack you must give way to a boat close hauled on starboard tack.
3. If you are to windward of another boat sailing in the same direction you must keep out of the way.
4. If you have a wind aft of your boat you must keep out of the way of all other sailing craft.
5. If you are overtaking another vessel (sail or power) you must keep out of the way.
6. Power craft give way to sail, but a sailing vessel does not have the right to hamper, in a narrow channel, the safe passage of a power-driven vessel which can navigate only inside such channel.

In your early days you may decide to keep out of the way of everything and this is always my advice to beginners. You may remember the lines someone wrote of the pedestrian who started over the road crossing without looking:

> He was right, dead right, as he toddled along,
> But he's just as dead as if he was wrong.

Perhaps the least heeded of the 'Rules of the Road' is number 27: *Special Circumstances* which reads: 'In obeying and construing these Rules, due regard shall be had to all dangers of navigation and collision, and any special circumstances, *including the limitations of the craft involved*, which may render a departure from the above Rules necessary in order to avoid immediate danger' (my italics).

This means that you must not expect a deep draught sailing boat to give way to your light draught sailing dinghy if by doing so it will run aground. There must be reasonable give and take, and an appreciation of other helmsmen's problems. Nor must you imagine that power craft are manoeuvrable under all circumstances: many of them become difficult to steer at low speeds when the wind is blowing from the beam, for the reason that sometimes seven-eighths of the side of the boat is out of the water. The excessive leeway caused cannot be offset except by speeding up the engine.

If you find yourself on a starboard tack, running into shallow water and shut in by another boat going in the same direction you will be quite in order to call for water as a preliminary to turning on to port tack. This is one of dozens of examples where Rule 27 comes into operation.

Small boat helmsmen are especially pig-headed about the right of way of sail over power. In one estuary I know well a large ferry moves up every half hour, dinghies tacking heedlessly across its bow, their helmsmen repeating to themselves: 'Power gives way to sail.' These particular ferries have the profile of a block of flats, the windage on their sides is enormous, and there is very little depth to spare on either side: and still their captains are as considerate as possible. Helmsmen must reciprocate unless they are to earn the hostility of merchant skippers.

It is well to remember that a large power vessel cannot be stopped in its tracks by reversing engines. A large liner or tanker may take as much as a mile to stop from full speed ahead.

Power vessels overtaking sailing craft frequently alter course to avoid interference and signal their intentions by sounding a siren:

1. One short blast means: 'I am turning to starboard.'
2. Two short blasts mean: 'I am turning to port.'
3. Three short blasts mean: 'My engines are going full speed astern.' But do not forget that this does not mean that the vessel is not still carrying forward way.

In some crowded waterways such as the Thames 'the ordinary practice of seamen' departs from the Rules governing sound signals and if you sail in such an area you must learn the local rules if you are to keep out of trouble.

Sooner or later you will find yourself making a passage at night in which you will meet other vessels. Your own craft should carry the following:

1. A white light at the stern to show $67\frac{1}{2}°$ on either side of

the fore-and-aft line, and visible for at least two miles in clear weather.

2. Green starboard and red port lights, each so fixed as to show only from right ahead to $22\frac{1}{2}°$ abaft the beams on the respective sides, and visible for at least two miles in clear weather.

If by reason of heavy weather or on account of other sufficient cause these navigation lights cannot be displayed, they must be kept close at hand for showing to other vessels approaching. Most yachtsmen have ready a powerful flashlight: beamed on to the sails it may well save you from near heart failure on your first night passage.

If you have to anchor in an area where there is a possibility of movement by other vessels during hours of darkness a white light should be displayed from the forepart so as to be visible at a distance of at least two miles in clear weather all round the horizon. But if you want a sound sleep try to find a quiet anchorage where the wash from the early morning ferry will not throw you out of your warm bunk.

More complex regulations apply to vessels of 40 tons (gross registered) and since you will certainly not be owning a craft of that size, they are omitted.

Probably the best way of applying the Rules of the Road at night is to learn the rather badly scanning jingle:

When both side lights you see ahead,
Port your helm and show your red:
But green to green, or red to red,
Means perfect safety – go ahead.

If to your starboard red appear
It is your duty to keep clear:
To act as judgment says is proper,
To port – or starboard – back – or stop her.

But when upon your port is seen
A steamer's starboard light of green
There's not much for you to do,
For green to port keeps clear of you.

Both in safety and in doubt
Always keep a good look out:
In danger, with no room to turn,
Ease her, stop her, go astern.

In a dinghy at night, whether sailing, rowing or under outboard engine, keep a flashlight at hand to signal your presence to other craft.

Planning a Passage

Dead reckoning is the basis of coastal navigation and it involves taking into account the different factors which help or hinder a yacht making a passage. Some of these are estimates and some can be measured or checked: much that is planned can be altered by a change in the direction or speed of the wind, but the essential is that you must always know your position. This means that you must seize every chance of taking any sort of observation which will confirm your reckoning.

In laying a course you will have to take into account the speed of your boat through the water, the effects of tidal currents and the leeway which it makes on any given point of sailing. The first and second of these can be plotted with reasonable accuracy and the third can only come from knowledge of your boat. Let us work out two examples:

Figure 22 shows the magnetic track between 'A' and 'B' and there is a tidal current at 230° of 2 knots. From the compass rose draw a line at 230° magnetic to join AB and measure off 2 miles to the point T. You estimate your speed through the water as 4 knots: setting the dividers to measure off 4 miles and with T as the centre, cut AB at C. The resultant CT taken off the compass rose by the parallel rule gives the course to steer to make good the track AB as 71°. Speed over the ground is 2·4 knots.

Figure 23 calculates a course to steer given a tidal current of the same 2 knot force, but now favourably abaft the beam, and the same estimated speed through the water.

Naturally if the tidal current comes from dead astern or

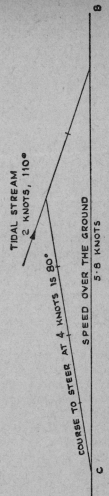

TIDAL STREAM
2 KNOTS, 110°

COURSE TO STEER AT 4 KNOTS IS 80°

SPEED OVER THE GROUND
5·8 KNOTS

FIGURE 23 Calculating course to steer

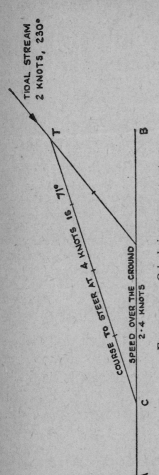

TIDAL STREAM
2 KNOTS, 230°

COURSE TO STEER AT 4 KNOTS IS 71°

SPEED OVER THE GROUND
2·4 KNOTS

FIGURE 22 Calculating course to steer

dead ahead all that you will have to do is to add or subtract its speed from speed through the water.

It must be clear that these are examples of calculations only, to be corrected by measurement and observation: if the log shows the speed through the water to be 6 knots instead of 4 the course to be steered will alter. Wherever possible bearings of conspicuous landmarks will be taken with the hand-bearing compass to give a timed position to be marked on the chart.

These are simple cases in which your boat has a fair wind enabling you to steer a course without the need for averaging out the track distance covered if you have to tack from A to B, and this is exactly the sort of voyage which you should try to plan as your first venture in coastal navigation. Your timing must also be such that you get the best possible advantage from the tidal sets which will help you on your way and if you can arrange to arrive in a strange anchorage on a rising tide, so much the better.

The plans for your first voyage between ports must be laid on the eve of a suitable day. By this I mean that you will need to have all the conditions with you, for many a sailing career has foundered on the statement: 'Tomorrow we'll go to Cowes.' If you qualify this by: 'all being well', you will be wise, and wiser still, if there is any doubt about the weather, if you decide to stay on your mooring. Set a maximum of 25 miles on your first voyage.

You have got your charts, instruments and tide-tables together; a northerly wind of Force 3 to 4 favouring your course to the westward is forecast. You will start by drawing a line on your chart between your point of departure and your destination, these usually being buoys or leading marks off each harbour.

Lay the parallel rule against the track line drawn on the chart and 'walk' the rule across the chart to the nearest compass rose. With the edge of the rule passing through the centre of the rose read off the *magnetic* bearing (272°) and make a note of it.

Since the distance between ports is not great you will be

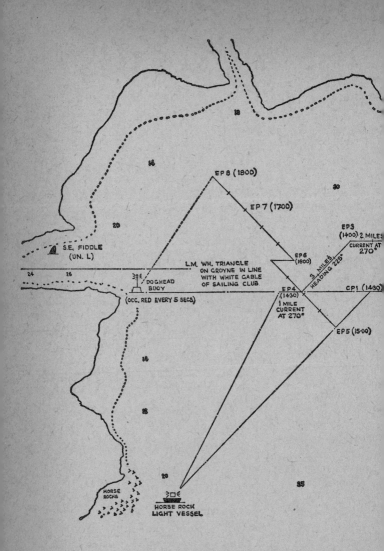

FIGURE 24 Coastal chart: Bar Buoy to Doghead Buoy

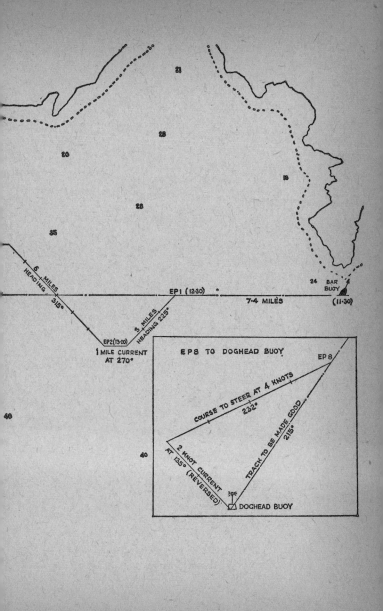

21

28

26

19

23

35

6 MILES
HEADING
315°

EP1 (12·30)

7·4 MILES

24 BAR
BUOY

(11·30)

3 MILES
HEADING 225°

EP2 (13·00)
1 MILE CURRENT
AT 270°

48

40

EP8 TO DOGHEAD BUOY

EP 8

COURSE TO STEER AT 4 KNOTS
232°

TRACK TO BE MADE GOOD
215°

2 KNOT CURRENT
AT 135° (REVERSED)

315°

DOGHEAD BUOY

able to work on one coastal chart and a harbour plan. Your track will take you across a deeply indented bay and you will be out of sight of land for most of the voyage, which means that your progress and position must be worked out by dead reckoning with no buoys or landmarks by which to make a check. At some point you should sight the Horse Rock Lightship and this will help to check your position. Your real objective is Doghead Buoy and from here you will be able to pick out the two leading marks which, if brought into line, will guide you into the anchorage.

Measuring the distance to be covered with the dividers and the scale you find that it is exactly 25 nautical miles. In your home waters you will have got a fair idea of the speed through the water you can expect on a reach in the Force 4 wind forecast and you estimate this at 5 knots, or 5 hours from your point of departure at the Bar Buoy to the entrance at your destination. But what about the tide?

From the tidal stream data on the chart you find that you can expect a west-going tide of 2 knots for the first three hours after low water, reducing to 1 knot for the next hour, becoming east-going at 1 knot for the following hour and then running from the north-west (135°) for the next five hours at 2 knots. A brief calculation shows you that if you sail at low water you can expect to finish the voyage of 25 miles in four hours at the most, in which time the wind will have moved you 20 miles and the tide another 7. You have, in fact, time in hand, for a more detailed calculation will show your estimated time between buoys as about 3 hrs 40 mins. You arrive at this figure by taking the total distance you expect to cover in 4 hours (20 miles plus 7 miles from the tidal stream) dividing the result by 4 to get an hourly average, which is in turn divided into the mileage to be covered. Calculating that low tide will be at 11.30 on the morrow, your crew is warned to be on hand to go off in the tender at 10.30. By the time you have stowed provisions, made sail and got outside the harbour to the Bar Buoy the west-going tide will have started to run.

Executing the Plan

The morrow should hold no fears for you and if the 06.45 Shipping Forecast says something rather cautious about the wind backing westerly later, what of it?

As the day goes on you are going to appreciate that 'later' is a term elastic enough to mean 'soon'.

Having cleared your home port the patent log is streamed at the Bar Buoy and the time noted. The track you want to make good is the course to be steered, since no allowance has to be made for a cross-tide which would drift you off it. Your boat should make no leeway on a reach. The deviation card for your compass shows that you must allow for 2° W *to be applied clockwise (steer 274° magnetic:) if it had read 2° E it would have been applied anti-clockwise (steer 270° magnetic).* So 274° it is and if you can tear yourself away from the chart-table you may as well go below and make some coffee for the crew.

When you come on deck again the Bar Buoy has become a distant dot and the shores you know so well are only a hazy line. Some other yachts are about, one tacking towards your home port, wearing a yellow 'Q' flag to show that she has come from a foreign port and requires clearance. You may even feel a little lonely: the responsibility is all yours and you recall that planning is one thing and execution another. If you are old enough you may even recall the wartime cynicism: 'Somebody threw a planner in the works.' But you feel rather a dashing fellow.

At the end of the first hour you read the log at 5·4 nautical miles, and this plus another 2 miles from the tidal stream puts you 7·4 miles on your way – almost a third of it. You are justifiably cheerful as you mark EP.1 as your position on the chart at 12.30: everything is going for you and you ought to be on an anchor and all snugged down in a couple of hours or so at this rate. At this rate . . .

But this rate does not continue, unhappily. Ten minutes ago you noticed that both foresail and main needed sheeting in although you were dead on course. Some of the upper cloud appears to have a drift from west to east and you recall the early morning forecast of a back in the wind. You know that you may expect an increase in wind strength as it backs and you now have a decision to make.

According to all the signs from the upper cloud the surface wind will shortly be heading you by blowing at 270°, straight along the line of your track. You will have to tack and this will double the distance to be sailed. Against this the freshening wind will take you faster through the water, and the tide still runs to the westward for another three hours.

Most probably it will not enter your head to turn away downwind and sail back to your home port, even though this might be the most comfortable, perhaps the most prudent course. Go to 'B' you have said you will, so go to 'B' it is.

In a matter of minutes the wind draws dead ahead and you find yourself sailing closehauled to starboard on a heading of 225° and this is as close as you can get to the mean course of 272°. Your new plan must be worked out.

If you sail for 30 minutes on the present starboard tack and for 60 minutes on a port tack, a final 30 minutes on starboard tack should put you back on to the mean course line and at a point where you might be able to get a bearing on the Horse Rock Lightship. At the end of 30 minutes you have logged 3 miles on a heading of 225° and you go about on to port tack and a heading of 315°. Your second estimated position at EP.2 is thus 3 miles along the 225° line and 1 mile along the 270° current line. The 60 minute port tack shows 6 miles logged and 2 miles allowance for current at 270° to position you at EP.3. The 30 minute starboard tack (if you log 3 miles) plus the 1 mile current allowance should put you on the mean course line at EP.4 and from this point the Horse Rock Lightship should bear 210°, if you see it at all.

After 25 minutes you sight Horse Rock but dead ahead bearing 225° instead of 210° fine on the port bow. Something has gone wrong: since you have only one bearing you cannot make an accurate fix but you can safely assume that you are pretty well on the mean course line, and from the lightship position on the chart you rule off a line at 45° – the reciprocal of your 225° bearing. Where this cuts the mean course line you mark the corrected position at CP.1.

You decide to hold on to the starboard tack, still able to keep a heading of 225° without pinching, whilst you have a brief mental inquest. CP.1 puts you 15·8 miles on the way, against the EP.4 position – 19·8 miles towards B. From knowledge of your boat you are sure that you cannot have made enough leeway to account for the error. The most probable explanation is that the tide has not run as strongly to the west as you expected. You decide that at the end of the starboard tack you will make no allowance for tide (since it seems to be turning early) and that you will make your next port tack one of 180 minutes, plotting your hourly positions on the assumption of a current running at 90° for 1 hour and 135° for the next 2 hours. When you go about at EP.5 at 15.00 Horse Rock still bears 225°, so you have lost nothing to leeward. This confirms your belief that the west-going current has not carried for as long as predicted and it can be assumed that the tidal current at 1 knot to 90° will start to run earlier than the forecast time of 15.30.

In the next hour you log 4 miles and a 1 mile allowance for tide puts you at EP.6 at 16.00. You note that your speed through the water has fallen as you come under the shelter of the land. There are 12 miles of deep water ahead and if you hold your port tack for 2 further hours the tidal current will be coming from dead ahead. You have plenty of sea room and you hold your course.

At 17.00 you have done rather better through the water than you expected by logging 5 miles, and allowing 2 miles for current you mark your estimated position at EP.7. An hour later a log reading of 4 miles and a deduction of 2 miles for current puts you at EP.8. There is a considerable amount of murk ahead as evening begins to fall and you can see some distant lights on high ground.

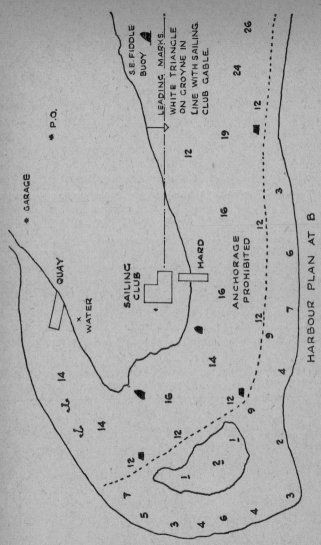

FIGURE 25 Harbour plan

If your position at EP.8 is correct Doghead Buoy bears at 215°. Even with a tide under the starboard quarter you estimate that you can lay the buoy on the next starboard tack and you must work out a course to steer. You can do this either on your chart or on scrap paper.

As data you have a 4 knot estimate of speed through the water, a 2 knot tide at 135° and a track to make good of 215°. On any convenient scale (that of the chart if you are working on it) lay off a track line at 215° and from any point on it lay off the current at 135°. Mark off 2 miles on the current line *in the reverse direction to the movement* and from that point with a radius of 4 miles (speed through the water) cut the track line and complete the triangle, the third side giving the course to steer to make good the desired track (see inset in Fig. 24).

The wind has begun to veer a little to the north and you are able to hold the heading of 232°. A measurement of the track line gives you 3·7 miles to cover and at 4 knots you should see Doghead (Occ. Red ev. 5 secs.) in about 50 minutes.

After 45 minutes, incredibly, the red light comes up, dowsing for a second every five seconds. Even the wind helps by continuing to veer round to the north to give you an easy sail into harbour. You've made it.

This is the kind of difference which you will experience between plans as laid and as executed, for wind changes will dictate fresh calculations and timings. Read about the subject, which cannot be dealt with at length in this book: Commander M. J. Rantzen's *Coastal Navigation Wrinkles* is a first-class guide.

Set yourself some problems with a chart and tide-tables. Let your first port-to-port sail not be too ambitious and make no bones about returning to your home port if the wind heads you. After all, you're doing this for fun.

CHAPTER 7

RACING

Racing Rules – Preparation for Racing

THIS is a subject which can only be briefly discussed here. You will learn more about getting the best from your boat by racing than by anything else. This is particularly so if you own a one-design, where the skill of the helmsman is the main factor in finishing first over the line. Against this will be your disinclination to make an ass of yourself or the feeling that you will be in the way of more experienced helmsmen. Or you may simply prefer to sail off for the uncomplicated pleasure of a picnic and a swim.

Whatever your decision, it must be shaped by the fact that you sail for pleasure. If you are building up a fine set of stomach ulcers by worrying over your work during the week there is little point in starting off another set by worrying about racing at weekends. Clubs very naturally like to have a good turnout for races which need considerable organization, and some of them even tend to adopt the line of: 'If you aren't going to race we don't want you.'

This is much to be regretted and the more usual attitude is to encourage new owners and members to try racing in suitable weather. You will find that if you declare an interest in racing another member will be glad to initiate you by asking you to crew for him, and this is your best course.

If you sail on the confined waters of a flooded gravel pit you are practically bound to end up by racing because there is little else to do. This is something you must bear in mind when deciding on your base.

It is difficult to judge whether husbands and wives should race together as a crew. Some combinations work very well: others, less well. I asked one wife how it worked with her and she said: 'Wonderfully, now. But at first it was awful. Nag, nag, nag. Inquests after every race – the lot! Then one day I just couldn't take any more, so I jumped overboard and swam ashore.'

'But now?' I asked.

'Wonderful. He says: "Well done, darling" after every race and if we win I get a box of chocolates.'

So this is a decision you must take for yourself. In teaching sailing I usually separate husbands and wives; if there is just that tiny tendency toward back-seat driving . . .

Racing Rules

A set of Rules came into force in 1961 which now govern racing all over the world. Prior to this there were many and wide differences in various codes and the whole situation is now much simplified. It is outside the scope of this book to list and explain the Rules, copies of which may be obtained from most of the chandlers or direct from the Royal Yachting Association, 171 Victoria Street, London, S.W.1. A very clear explanation of the Rules is given in Hugh Somerville's *The Yacht Racing Rules Simplified* (Adlard Coles, 5s.).

It is the custom of the sea that yachts which are not racing shall keep clear of those that are. In some circles this is construed as meaning that craft which are racing have a right of way over all other craft, but this is a matter of a courtesy, not of a right. Where the Rules conflict with the ordinary Rules of the Road the latter will take precedence, and this may govern your insurance company's decision in meeting a claim should you be in collision with a boat which is racing.

Elsewhere I have mentioned the racing flag: square in form, the R.Y.A. requires that it shall be worn at the top of the mast while racing and that it shall be capable of being lowered while under way.

There is a tendency for boats which race a good deal to wear the square racing flag under all circumstances. To do so, with the implied request to all other craft to keep clear, is sheer bad manners.

You will hear much talk of protests after races and this may discourage you from joining in. It is a fact that there is a school of thought which works upon the lines of: 'If I can't finish first, how can I eliminate the chap who did?'

This sort of Rulesmanship can sour the atmosphere when it is taken too far and I know of clubs where practically no member speaks to another after racing, so thick is the air with pending protests. The practitioner of Rulesmanship will tell you that there is an obligation upon you to protest if there are grounds to do so, but nothing in the Rules requires this. A private rule which I recommend to you is that you should not protest unless your own position in the race is affected by the wrongful action of another helmsman.

Preparation for Racing

John Illingworth has said and written that a race is more than half won before the start. This is very true: the preparation of the boat is extremely important. The bottom must be clean and smooth to reduce friction through the water, rigging must be set up so that the sails drive the boat at her best speed and where the Class Rules allow of it all superfluous weight is stripped.

The crew itself must be in reasonable physical trim even for dinghy racing. If you have the luck to get some ocean racing you will find your skipper requiring you to sign the pledge some days before the start, for you are in for a tough time.

Your tactics during a race, particularly in a tideway or river, will largely depend on the weather and ten minutes' thoughtful study of the course to be sailed should help you to find the best of the wind and current.

This is a subject in itself and the classic work is Ian Proctor's *Racing Dinghy Sailing* (Adlard Coles, 16s.). A sister book by the same author is *Racing Dinghy Maintenance* (Adlard Coles, 16s.).

CHAPTER 8

TYPES OF SAILING CRAFT

Hard-chine Plywood – Hot- and Cold-moulded
Dinghies – Catamarans and Trimarans – Glass Fibre
Dinghies – Clinker-built Dinghies – Keelboats (Day-
sailers) – Sailing Cruisers – Cruising Catamarans

I AM not going to attempt in this chapter to offer advice about the sort of boat you should buy, for eventual ownership will surely be in your thoughts. That follows in the next chapter: this is simply a review of types commonly found in Britain.

There are six main types of construction:

Hard-chine hulls built in marine plywood.

Hot- or cold-moulded hulls built on formers from layers of thin wood.

Glass fibre craft.

Clinker, in which the hull planking overlaps.

Carvel, where planks of the hull are laid edge to edge.

Metal hulls in which plates of either light alloy, steel or black iron are welded or riveted together. There are no established classes of metal hulled sailing dinghies.

All have their pros and cons and the novice is bewildered by the multiplicity of types: confusion grows as he begins to talk to owners, for all are fierce protagonists of the type of boat which they happen to sail.

All craft can be divided into those which derive from working boats and those designed for pleasure use. The Thames and larger coastal barges were built for seaworthiness, ease of handling and economy of crew. Much of the rigging puzzles the small-boat sailor but it works admirably. The same applies to fishing craft, the Morecambe Bay prawners, the Colchester oyster-dredging smacks and the beautiful square-transomed West Country craft. Many of these have become fine yachts capable of staying at sea in all weathers and not a few designers go back to them for inspiration. Most impressive in their sea behaviour are the fine double-ended Fife-type motor yachts based so closely on traditional fishing boat design.

A firm believer that the aspirant should start his sailing in a dinghy, let us see how it has developed. The word, by the way, is not even English in origin: the Bombay bumboatman sculling his craft alongside the anchored craft calls it a 'Dinghee' and one supposes the term (and perhaps an example of the boat) was imported by some long-forgotten East Indiaman. The first sailing dinghies were in the traditional terms of clinker-built fishing boats strong enough to be launched from a beach. They were heavy craft embodying a shallow-draught keel and the few who sailed them usually followed the advice of a local boat-builder on design matters.

In the early years of the century the centreboard dinghy began to appear in some strength and it was sometimes carvel built for improved performance. Local classes sprang up and the sport of dinghy sailing became somewhat like the Eton Wall Game: you could always play it among yourselves but when it came to sailing against other clubs some handicap system had to be worked out.

Although a few of these ancient classes survive precariously they tend to be swamped by the tremendous increase in the numbers of one-design and restricted-design dinghies.

'One design' means that all boats in the class are identical and helmsmen race on rigidly equal terms. Any departure from constructional and measurement rules means automatic disqualification and boats are not eligible to race unless the entrant can produce a certificate from a qualified measurer. Most classes also insist upon an annual buoyancy test.

'Restricted design' means that there is a certain latitude in modifying and improving a design. The designers not unnaturally say that this improves the breed, but it also means that boats become dated fairly quickly. In some classes the really keen helmsman buys a new boat every year: he has to if he wants to keep a really impressive array of silver cups about the house.

Today clinker and carvel boats are still built, but in decreasing numbers. A lack of craftsmen and the consequent high cost is one of the factors, although the glued clinker boats which have recently appeared may halt the retreat.

The traditionally built boat is inevitably on the decline and this is sad. Planks cut, shaped and put together by craftsmen will always show a fragmentary trace of their origins and of the men who built the boat.

By the end of the Second World War a lack of metals had brought laminated wood sheeting into use. These laminates of thin wood were sometimes moulded into shape and glued together, either cold or under heat and pressure. The ordinary flat plywood known before the war had been vastly improved by the new water-resistant glues.

Fairey Marine began to make a large range of hot-moulded boats and are today the third largest hull producers in the world. Designers of the stature of Uffa Fox were responsible for the Firefly, Jollyboat and a host of other craft built under the hot-moulding system. Sailing cruisers, the *Atalanta*, the *Titania* and the *Fulmar* soon became familiar sights round the shores of Britain: a power-craft range appeared and is still being developed.

At the same time many designers began to use flat sheets of the new special marine plywoods. The first of these to make a lasting impression was Jack Holt with his G.P.14, which broke new ground in building techniques. In place of overlapping or edge-to-edge planking, sheets of shaped plywood, strengthened by ribs and stringers glued and screwed along the chines, dictated a new shape of hull. Light and strong, it was capable of high planing speeds: kits for the home builder were mass-produced, professional boat-builders adopted the new techniques and plywood chine boats soon outnumbered the conventionally designed craft by at least ten to one. Ian Proctor designed his brilliant Wayfarer, Gull and Zenith. Jack Holt's Enterprise today tops 10,000 sail-numbers.

Towards the end of the war some experiments began with the use of moulded shapes, not only for boats, using laminates of synthetic resins reinforced with woven glass fibre. This type of construction has the advantage that whilst the material cost is high the labour cost is low since a high proportion of the work is semi-skilled.

The first results were not encouraging: builders tried to make the expensive material go further by mixing cheap 'fillers', with poor results and many failures. The emergence of the glass fibre reinforced hull as a most serious competitor with wooden craft is probably mainly due to the patient work of Halmatic Ltd. of Portsmouth. Unusually farsighted, the Halmatic factory is open to the inspection of other builders: a poor example of glass fibre construction gives the material a bad name generally.

Next to fishing craft small boats used by the Admiralty came in for the hardest wear of any. For some years various experimental hulls and types of glass fibre construction have been under rigorous Admiralty tests in everyday conditions and in all climates. The conclusions reached were that far less maintenance is needed as compared with timber craft and that where the requirement for a number of boats justifies the cost of a mould, all future Admiralty boats up to 27 ft in length will be built in glass-reinforced plastic.

The glass fibre boat requires the absolute minimum of maintenance and herein lies much of its attraction. Surface scratches on the hull can be erased and, given the same care during a season as would be accorded to a painted or varnished boat, little needs to be done after laying up. The amount of wood trimming is usually small and perhaps two hours cleaning down and varnishing of these parts is all that is needed. Certainly the laborious hours of scraping, filling and painting have vanished for the owner of a glass fibre hull.

Should the boat be holed a quick repair can be effected by an amateur and without much loss of sailing time.

The glass fibre hull is here to stay and the annual increase in the number appearing at the National Boat Show is significant. There is prejudice against the material, usually from those without any experience of it. Vested interests have much to say against it and this is not unnatural when many builders have heavy capital investments in woodworking machinery. Glass fibre makes a good boat and my main feeling about it is that it is, like any other man-made product, an unsympathetic material. The feel, the sight, the touch and the smell of wood are as pleasing as natural silk is compared to man-made fibres.

Metal hulls have much to commend them and an increasing number of small runabouts, mostly powered by outboard engines, are being built in light alloys. There appear to be no sailing dinghies using the material but some attractive small keel boats of five tons or so are being built in Holland. As with fibreglass, annual maintenance is a fairly easy affair, many of the hulls being used unpainted.

Larger yachts built up from steel plates riveted or welded together also come chiefly from Holland. A steel hull calls for considerable annual maintenance and in this respect has no advantages over wood.

These are the principal methods of construction and some of the types in each category are reviewed. The sailing dinghies grouped into the differing constructional methods come first, then the catamarans. The keel boats and cruising catamarans follow irrespective of the material or method of construction.

The standing of a designer means much and many fine dinghies have come from the drawing-boards of Uffa Fox, Jack Holt, Ian Proctor and Thomas Kirby, to name only a few: younger men such as John Mace are beginning to make their marks, and the name of the designer will do much to commend a boat to you.

Many craft are designed and copyrighted by the Press, notably the *Yachting Monthly* and the *Yachting World*. Ian Proctor's remarkable little SigneT is sponsored by the *Sunday Times*. Backing of this order is valuable since the reputation of the sponsor is involved. The weight of publicity given to a new class almost guarantees that the boat will become popular and so maintain a high secondhand price.

Hard-chine Plywood

By far the most popular type of construction because it eases the problem of home-building, the review which follows is roughly in order of size.

International Cadet

Overall length: 10′ 6¾″	Beam 4′ 2″
Waterline length: 9′ 3″	Sail area: 55 sq. ft
Designer: Jack Holt	Buoyancy: Air-bag or built-in
Rig: Bermudan	Builder: Several, in all parts of the world

Group-Captain E. F. Haylock inspired Jack Holt to design this junior-class boat in 1948 and more than 3,500 have been built in twenty-six countries. Not long ago Group-Captain Haylock remarked to me that it was more of an international movement than a class and so it is: crews come even from behind the Iron Curtain to the annual week of racing at Burnham-on-Crouch.

The basic ideas behind the design were that it should be easily within the capabilities of young crews to build from scratch or assemble from a kit in a school workshop or the home. It had to have the sailing qualities of a good racing boat and it had to be safe. The project succeeded brilliantly and the names of many helmsmen who today steer more powerful craft are engraved on the *Yachting World* Cadet Trophy – clear evidence of the sound grounding in handling a miniature racing boat.

The sail plan includes a spinnaker which pulls the boat along well downwind without being so large that it could be dangerous if unwisely set in a brisk blow.

Weighing about 150 lb. the Cadet can be carried on the top of most small cars. The price differs slightly between builders but is about £180 complete with sails.

Gull

Overall length: 11′	Beam: 4′ 9″
Waterline length: 10′ 6″	Sail area: 70 sq. ft
Designer: Ian Proctor	Buoyancy: Built-in
Rig: Gunter	Builders: Small Craft of Southampton Ltd. and some licensed builders

A sturdy little dinghy which can be sailed, rowed or pushed along by a small outboard, the Gull has introduced hundreds of families to the sea. A feature which particularly commends it is that all the buoyancy is built-in. The short spars and mast can be stowed within the hull and this makes for convenient car-stop transport.

In spite of the fact that the class is built only by the copyright holders, a limited number of licensed builders and from kits, sail-numbers are over the thousand mark.

For no particular reason I sailed a Gull in November of 1958 round the Isle of Wight. Going eastabout from Bembridge I made Yarmouth in the first day, stayed the night and completed the circuit on the following day. I used the bailer twice only – in the chop at St Catherine's race and at the Needles – and the trip confirmed my belief in the Gull as a splendid little sea boat.

The hull weighs 172 lb. and the cost with sails is about £220 complete.

Heron (Car top)

Overall length: 11′ 3″	Beam: 4′ 6″
Waterline length: 11′	Sail area: 70 sq. ft
Designer: Jack Holt	Buoyancy: Air-bag
Rig: Gunter	Builders: Several

Primarily designed as a small transportable boat needing no trailer, the Heron has grown into a class of formidable size. All spars can be stowed and lashed within the hull: two adults find no difficulty in hoisting the boat on to the roof rack of a small car.

The idea of sailing from different bases is attractive and

eliminates many of the early problems which beset the new-comer. The Heron can be rowed or propelled by a small out-board and is often used as a tender to larger yachts.

The hull weighs about 150 lb. and the cost is about £220 complete with sails.

SigneT

Overall length: 12′ 5″	Beam: 4′ 9″
Waterline length: 11′ 6″	Sail area: 88 sq. ft
Designer: Ian Proctor	Buoyancy: Built-in
Rig: Bermudan	Builders: Several

The unusual spelling of the type-name indicates that this boat was sponsored by the *Sunday Times*. Intended for young people and those buying a first boat, it is also a stepping-stone between older types of sailing dinghy and the modern planing boat.

Ian Proctor set out to produce a design which should be supremely easy to build at home without any special skills. The plans are full scale and so can be stuck to timber or ply-wood before cutting out.

Flat-bottomed for cheapness and ease of construction, the SigneT is not one of the most beautiful designs when seen out of the water. But she goes like a dream and outsails dinghies costing twice as much. So much buoyancy is built into her that there is rarely any water to bale out after a capsize. Four SigneTs sailed the channel in July 1963.

The weight is about 150 lb. and the cost about £180 com-plete with sails. This is the cheapest thoroughbred boat there is and the sail-numbers are building up spectacularly.

Graduate

Overall length: 12′ 6″	Beam: 4′ 6″
Waterline length: 12′	Sail area: 83·5 sq. ft
Designer: Dick Wyche	Buoyancy: Built-in
Rig: Bermudan	Builders: Several

This lively one-design racing boat was sponsored by *Light Craft* in 1952 and has now introduced many hundreds of helmsmen and crews to the handling of a high performance planing dinghy.

A little more difficult to build than some boats, many hundreds have nevertheless been built from kits by amateurs.

The weight is 170 lb. and the cost about £190 complete with sails.

'Yachting World' Solo

Overall length: 12′ 4½″	Beam: 4′ 11″
Waterline length: 12′	Sail area: 90 sq. ft (Racing rig)
	63 sq. ft (Cruising rig)
Designer: Jack Holt	Buoyancy: Built-in
Rig: Una Bermudan	Builders: Several

A single-hander dinghy (Finn) is now an international and Olympic class and the Solo was sponsored by the *Yachting World* in order to bring on potential Olympic helmsmen. In fact many a Solo owner has gone straight into it from a Cadet.

An exciting boat to handle, the fully battened single sail is very responsive to adjustments to suit the wind of the day. The Solo planes easily and rights readily on capsize: the buoyancy margin is high.

Whilst the Solo is always raced single-handed it is not so anti-social a boat as might be supposed. Under either cruising or racing rig there is ample room for two adults.

The hull weighs about 150 lb. and the cost, including sails, about £240.

'Yachting World' Vagabond

Overall length: 11′ 9″	Beam: 4′ 9″
Waterline length: 11′ 3″	Sail area: 87 sq. ft
Designer: Jack Holt	Buoyancy: Built-in
Rig: Gunter	Builders: Several

The Vagabond was the logical follow up from the Heron. Slightly larger overall (and it is surprising how much difference a few inches make), it is still light enough to be hoisted on a car-top rack by two adults. There is room for two adults and two children under sail, more if the boat is used with an outboard engine.

The class is vigorous in its promotion and is growing in France as well as Britain.

The hull weighs about 170 lb. and the cost is about £250 complete with sails.

National Enterprise

Overall length : 13′ 3″	Beam : 5′ 3″
Waterline length : 12′ 9″	Sail area : Cruising 80 sq. ft
	Racing 113 sq. ft
Designer : Jack Holt	Buoyancy : Air-bag
Rig : Bermudan	Builders : Numerous and world-wide

The now unhappily defunct *News Chronicle* commissioned Jack Holt to design a sailing dinghy of the widest possible appeal and the Enterprise was the result. Undoubtedly the support of a national newspaper did much to nourish the early growth of the class but it could not have failed to establish itself solely on its merits. Today there are 10,000 and the class is the fastest-growing in the world.

Probably 90 per cent of Enterprise helmsmen race their boats: the dinghy planes easily and is exhilarating to sail. For these reasons and the moderate cost younger people take to the boat eagerly.

The weight of the hull is about 200 lb. and the cost with sails about £270 (wood), £290 (glass fibre).

'Yachting World' G.P. 14

Overall length : 14′	Beam : 5′
Waterline length : 13′ 6″	Sail area : 102 sq. ft
Designer : Jack Holt	Buoyancy : Air-bag
Rig : Bermudan	Builders : Several

Sponsored by the *Yachting World* and designed by Jack Holt, G.P. stands for 'General Purpose'. It precisely describes the boat. Roomy and stable enough to accommodate two adults and two children without the overcrowding inevitable in a smaller boat, the G.P.14 has an enviable performance and great versatility. Unlike most of the sailing dinghies so far reviewed the G.P.14 will lie on moorings without swamping or blowing over in a gale and like most of the Holt family of boats can be rowed or outboarded – I have seen no fewer than eight aboard one so powered.

There is keen racing in the class at many centres both in Britain and abroad. But my guess is that probably half the G.P.14 owners are happy potterers, and more power to them.

The weight of the hull is about 285 lb. and the cost is about £310 (wood), £320 (glass fibre) complete with sails. The G.P.14 is normally transported by a road trailer.

Leader

Overall length: 14'	Beam: 5' 5"
Waterline length: 12' 11"	Sail area: 116 sq. ft
Designer: John Mace	Buoyancy: Built-in
Rig: Bermudan	Builders: Small Craft Blue Hulls Ltd. and licensed builders

There are many 14-ft sailing dinghies on the market and the Small Craft Design Team produced a boat which should improve on the stability characteristics of competitive craft and at the same time be faster. In the same way that the family car of today has the performance of the sports cars of five years ago, the equivalent development was overdue in dinghies. The Leader doubles brilliantly as a family dinghy and will make a mark in handicap racing.

The weight is about 235 lb. and the cost is about £310 complete with sails.

Zenith

Overall length: 14' 6"	Beam: 5' 10"
Waterline length: 13' 6"	Sail area: 127 sq. ft
Designer: Ian Proctor	Buoyancy: Built-in
Rig: Bermudan	Builders: Small Craft of Southampton Ltd. and licensed builders

Unmistakably an Ian Proctor design, the Zenith has continued to make steady progress since her introduction in 1960. She is a racing one-design thoroughbred built at a price much below that of the restricted classes from which are drawn the aristocrats of dinghy racing. Her performance is electrifying in a breeze and she moves in the lightest of airs.

One of the difficulties of establishing a one-design class is that owners always want to race against each other so that it is helmsman, not boats as such, which compete. This in turn means that clubs must be persuaded to adopt the class. It is bound to be uphill work with an out-and-out racing class but the Zenith is now officially adopted by a number of clubs.

The weight is about 200 lb. and the cost is about £250 complete with sails.

Wayfarer

Overall length: 15′ 10″   Beam: 6′ 1″
Waterline length: 14′ 10″ Sail area: 141 sq. ft
Designer: Ian Proctor   Buoyancy: Built-in
Rig: Bermudan   Builders: Small Craft Blue Hulls Ltd.
and licensed builders

I must at once confess that I am much prejudiced in favour of this splendidly sturdy dinghy, having sailed the type for probably more hours than any man alive. Roomy, stable and fast, she displays no vices of any kind. I have been caught in Force 7 blows and always felt that the boat was on my side and this is most comforting.

The class is built only by a few licensed builders who can measure up to the standards of the copyright owners but the sail-numbers are over 850. Very much a family boat, there is nevertheless keen racing in the class. Sailed two or three up for racing, there is ample room for four adults whilst cruising.

The boat is arranged so that two can sleep aboard under a camping cover in somewhat spartan conditions and many long coastal cruises in stages have been recorded. The most notable open sea achievements are three North Sea crossings to Denmark and Norway by Frank Dye, and in 1963 he sailed to Iceland.

The weight of the hull is about 365 lb. and the cost with sails about £420 (wood), £440 (glass fibre).

National Hornet

Overall length: 16′	Beam: 4′ 7″
Waterline length: 15′ 9″	Sail area: 121 sq. ft
Designer: Jack Holt	Buoyancy: Air bag
Rig: Bermudan	Builders: Several

Primarily a racing boat, the Hornet is seaworthy in a chop and tractable enough to be sailed by helmsmen of fairly limited experience. The dinghy embodies a sliding seat mounted on a bridge running athwartships. This enables the crew to get weight well outboard in comparative comfort and the management of the sliding seat whilst tacking is not so complicated as may be imagined.

Whilst the hull dimensions, sail area and rigging are strictly defined under the class rules there is considerable latitude in the arrangement of decking and buoyancy. Some hulls have sufficient excess of buoyancy to give 100 per cent self-draining of the cockpit. Glass fibre construction is allowable and a good example is built by Sail Craft Ltd. of Brightlingsea.

The hull weighs about 250 lb. and the cost is about £350 complete with sails.

Fireball

Overall length: 16′ 2″	Beam: 4′ 5″
Waterline length: 13′ 3″	Sail area: 123 sq. ft
Designer: Peter Milne	Buoyancy: Built-in
Rig: Bermudan	Builders: Chippendale Boats Ltd.

The class grows fast, because the Fireball illustrates a trend. Over the last few years several examples of what are best described as sailing surf-boards have appeared, most of them deriving from types sailed in warm climates. They did not seem to catch on in the chillier waters of our coasts, for at any sort of speed the crew is enveloped in clouds of spray.

The Fireball is the logical development of the sailing surfboard idea and, whilst giving a sizzling sail in a breeze, provides some shelter from spray with the well-rounded foredeck. From the appearance of the hull one might believe that she would not point well on the tack. In fact the Fireball points remarkably high.

The hull weighs about 175 lb. and the cost is about £300 complete with sails.

Hot- and Cold-moulded Dinghies

The difference between the two processes is that in the first layers of wood are glued together under pressure and then baked in large ovens: in the second little or no pressure is applied to the glued layers as they are shaped over a mould. In both cases the glues are specially developed for marine use and separation of the layers is impossible.

The principal British constructor of hot-moulded hulls is Fairey Marine Ltd. and the cold-moulded sailing dinghy has not established itself in any sort of numbers: some larger hulls are cold-moulded and are featured in the section covering cruising yachts. Boats are reviewed in order of size.

National Firefly

Overall length : 12′	Beam : 4′ 7″
Waterline length : 12′	Sail area : 90 sq. ft
Designer : Uffa Fox	Buoyancy : Built-in and air-bag
Rig : Bermudan	Builders : Fairey Marine Ltd.

More than 2,500 Fireflies sail in Britain, North America and the Middle East. The class continues to grow and is typical of the high quality and good secondhand value of the modern sailing dinghy. A recent Firefly Championship was won by an eleven-year-old boat, with a ten-year-old in second place. It is common for elderly craft to change hands at 90 per cent of the original price.

Quick to plane and easy to right if capsized, the Firefly is used almost exclusively for racing. There is nothing to prevent it being used for more docile everyday sailing.

The weight is about 205 lb. and the cost is about £250 complete with sails.

Albacore

Overall length: 15′   Beam: 5′ 4″
Waterline length: 15′   Sail area: 125 sq. ft
Designers: Fairey Marine   Buoyancy: Built-in or air-bag
        Design Team   Builders: Fairey Marine Ltd. and
Rig: Bermudan   others

The Albacore is described by its builders as a 'gentle thoroughbred'. There is room to carry two adults and two or three children combined with a good racing performance.

Not unlike a larger version of the Firefly in appearance, the class is one-design with some latitude in the rules. This has bred special Albacores in which buoyancy is built in, a turtle deck substituted for the standard flat deck and a centrally-sheeting horse built in. These refinements make for a faster boat with more crew space.

The hull weight is about 275 lb. and the cost is about £330.

Fairey Falcon Daysailer

Overall length: 16′ 6″   Beam: 5′ 11″
Waterline length: 15′ 6″   Sail area: 125 sq. ft
Designers: Fairey Marine   Buoyancy: Air-bag
        Design Team
Rig: Bermudan   Builders: Fairey Marine Ltd.

Six adults can sit inside this modern equivalent of the solid clinker-built dinghies once seen on the coasts of Britain. With a tough and fairly heavy hull built to take hard knocks the Falcon makes no pretension to great speed and is chiefly designed for family sailing in safety and comfort.

There is ample stowage room for camping gear and an outboard motor.

The weight of the hull is about 540 lb. and the cost is about £450 complete with sails.

Jollyboat

Overall length: 18′	Beam: 5′
Waterline length: 17′ 6″	Sail area: 150 sq. ft
Designer: Uffa Fox	Buoyancy: Air-bag and/or built-in
Rig: Bermudan	Builders: Fairey Marine Ltd.

Uffa Fox once had the ridiculous idea that he was growing older and needed a dinghy which would give him more room and a longer time to get across the boat when going about. It is typical of the man that he should then design the fastest normal boat in production.

Except in light winds the Jollyboat is usually raced with a crew of three, one of whom sits out to windward on the tacks in the canvas seat of the trapeze. This is a wire running to the top of the mast and the application of weight outboard helps to keep the boat upright. Speeds of 16 knots and a 10 knot average over a triangular course are common with the Jollyboat.

As with the Albacore the class rules give considerable latitude for modifications and few Jollyboats match each other except in hull dimensions, mast heights and sail areas.

The weight of the hull is about 300 lb. and the cost is about £460 complete with sails.

Catamarans and Trimarans

It always appears to me that there were faults in the original presentation of multi-hulled sailing craft. Too often they were described as being easy to sail, uncapsizeable and unsinkable. Instant sailing in the modern manner in fact. None of the designers and builders of serious intent would support these claims and the idea that a multi-hulled craft is bound to be best simply because it is multi-hulled is on the way out.

There is nothing particularly difficult in sailing these craft but they certainly differ from more conventional boats in some handling characteristics. And unless there is a special buoyancy device at the top of the mast they can present problems in righting if they capsize. Given enough wind any vessel can be so hove down that she goes over. As for being unsinkable, a hard enough knock will sink almost anything afloat.

Special difficulties exist in design. Putting it simply, the stresses on the bridge which unites the hulls are tremendous when one hull is perched on one wave and the other hull on another.

Multi-hulled craft take up a good deal of room in dinghy parks and on moorings and for this reason it may be difficult to find a base.

None of these observations imply an adverse criticism of catamarans or trimarans. Off the wind they give an electrifying sensation of speed and power. The acceleration of these light-draught hulls in a puff of wind has to be experienced to be believed. Some of their qualities of high performance should urge caution upon the novice: a believer in a claim that I have read: 'Absolutely no previous knowledge of sailing is necessary', could bring havoc to a crowded anchorage.

Some of the larger cruising catamarans are featured among the keel boats for convenience although their shallow draught does not properly qualify them for this category. What follows is a review in alphabetical order of those which belong among the sailing dinghies.

Cougar

Overall length: 18′ 9″	Beam: 7′ 11″
Waterline length: 17′	Sail area: 236 sq. ft
Designer: G. Prout & Sons Ltd	Buoyancy: Built-in
Rig: Bermudan	Builders: G. Prout & Sons Ltd.

The Cougar comes from a good stable. One of the many designs of the Prout brothers, the hulls are constructed in glass fibre and call for little maintenance. The boat handles well and is rated as the second fastest of the catamarans.

The weight is about 450 lb. and the cost is about £600 complete with sails.

Shark

Overall length: 20′   Beam: 10′
Waterline length: 17′ 6″   Sail area: 260 sq. ft or 222 sq. ft
Designer:
  J. R. Macalpine-Downie Buoyancy: Built-in
Rig: Bermudan   Builders: Sail Craft Ltd.

The width between the outer edges of each hull of a catamaran normally imposes an overall beam measurement which
occupies much valuable parking space. In the Shark the re-
moval of one bolt frees the bridge so that one hull folds on
top of the other, and the trailing width of 5′ is conveniently
small. No weakness is disclosed by its impressive racing results and the boat can be sailed either within the Shark one-
design limits of 260 sq. ft or in the I.Y.R.U. 'B' Class by
changing the sails.

The weight is about 350 lb. and the cost is about £650
complete with sails.

Shearwater

Overall length: 16′ 6″   Beam: 7′ 6″
Waterline length: 15′ 6″   Sail area: 160 sq. ft
Designer: G. Prout &   Buoyancy: Built-in
        Sons Ltd
Rig: Bermudan   Builders: G. Prout & Sons Ltd.

The largest catamaran class in the world, the Shearwater
has been under continuous development. The latest Mark III
is available in either plywood or glass fibre at roughly the
same price. When the Shearwater was introduced it at once
made a mark by its docility and speed and the boat is firmly
established as a family craft with an exhilarating performance.

The weight of the boat is about 370 lb. and the cost is
about £400 complete with sails.

Swift

Overall length: 14′ 6″   Beam: 5′ 10″
Waterline length: 13′ 6″   Sail area: 120 sq. ft

The ENTERPRISE, being raced here in Poole Harbour by the designer
Jack Holt and his wife

The JOLLYBOAT, a very fast dinghy here being ballasted to windward by the trapeze

The SOLO, a popular dinghy being sailed here by Jack Holt, the designer

The FIREFLY, a high performance racing dinghy here seen planing on a broad reach

Four SIGNETs, seen leaving St. Margaret's Bay for Calais which was reached 4½ hours later

Two ocean-racing yachts designed by Illingworth & Primrose
'Dambuster'   'Maica'

The Fairey FISHERMAN, a power boat which follows some traditional lines based on offshore fishing craft

The Dell Quay RANGER, a 25 ft. four-berth high speed luxury cruiser

Designer: G. Prout   Buoyancy: Built-in
       Sons Ltd.
Rig: Bermudan   Builders: G. Prout & Sons Ltd.

With the success of the Shearwater the Prout brothers rightly decided that there was a need for a smaller and lighter catamaran. The Swift is light enough to be carried on a cartop rack of special design. Not quite so fast as the Shearwater, this interesting boat is suitable for handling by a crew varying from one to four in number.

The weight of the boat is about 250 lb. and the cost is about £290 complete with sails.

Thai Mk.4

Overall length: 17′ 6″   Beam: 8′ 6″
Waterline length: 16′   Sail area: 215 sq. ft
Designer: Buoyancy: Built-in
  J. R. Macalpine-Downie
Rig: Bermudan   Builders: Sail Craft Ltd.

One of the characteristics of a good design is that the boat always appears to be smaller than it really is. Thai Mk.4 is beautifully proportioned and does not look her formidable 17′ 6″. Rated the fastest production catamaran, she has had a phenomenal success in racing and from the experience gained with her *Hellcat* was developed to beat the best boats America and Australia could produce.

The weight of the boat is about 275 lb. and the cost is about £500 complete with sails.

'Yachting World' Catamaran

Overall length: 15′ 6″   Beam: 7′
Waterline length: 14′ 9″   Sail area: 175 sq. ft
Designer: Buoyancy: Built-in
  J. R. Macalpine-Downie
Rig: Bermudan   Builders: Several

It took some time before the *Yachting World* decided to add a catamaran to their family of sponsored boats. Macalpine-Downie's Thai Mk.4 had been such an outstanding success that he was commissioned to design a boat that had to be fast, easy to sail and of a beam narrow enough to allow of easy trailing behind a small car. The class was an immediate success and upwards of three hundred have been built. The hulls may be either cold-moulded or built-in glass fibre.

The weight of the boat is about 260 lb. and the cost is about £330 complete with sails.

Glass Fibre Dinghies

Alpha

Overall length: 12′ 1″	Beam: 5′
Waterline length: 12′ 1″	Sail area: 90 sq. ft
Designer: Ian Proctor	Buoyancy: Moulded foam
Rig: Bermudan	Builders: Bossoms Boatyard Ltd.

So far as can be traced, the Alpha is the only sailing dinghy whose basic conception originated in the Engineering Faculty of a University – Oxford. The design was then taken over by Ian Proctor and the boat is now used for inter-university racing.

The Alpha bristles with new ideas: there is a synthetic rubber stem piece to soften the unintended ramming of another boat or a landing-stage and the integral foam buoyancy completely justifies the claim that she is unsinkable.

The weight of the hull is about 200 lb. and the cost is about £260 complete with sails.

Bosun

Overall length: 14′	Beam: 5′ 6″
Waterline length: 14′	Sail area: 115 sq. ft
Designer: Ian Proctor	Buoyancy: Moulded foam and built-in
Rig: Bermudan	Builders: Bossoms Boatyard Ltd.

The more mechanized the Royal Navy becomes the more interested it is in escaping into a sailing dinghy. When proposals were invited for a boat suitable for from two to four adults, having a minimum of maintenance needs and capable of being repaired without specialized knowledge, Ian Proctor drew upon the experience gained with the Alpha.

This interesting boat is unsinkable and the buoyancy reserves are enormous when compared with the size of the dinghy. When it comes to racing the Bosun is no sluggard and has inspired sufficient confidence in an owner for him to sail to France and back.

The weight of the hull is about 250 lb. and the cost is about £350 complete with sails.

Kestrel

Overall length: 15′ 7″	Beam: 5′ 4″
Waterline length: 15′ 1″	Sail area: 130 sq. ft
Designer: Ian Proctor	Buoyancy: Built-in
Rig: Bermudan	Builders: J. L. Gmach & Co.

The Kestrel was the first of several designs for execution in glass fibre from the drawing board of Ian Proctor: incorporating a special system of both built-in and expanded plastic buoyancy, the boat is practically unsinkable. The purpose of the design was to produce a stable family dinghy which would at the same time give a good account of itself in racing.

The weight of the hull is about 225 lb. and the cost is about £290 complete with sails.

Wineglass

Overall length: 15′	Beam: 5′ 10″
Waterline length: 14′	Sail area: 123 sq. ft (racing) or 98 sq. ft (cruising)
Designer: T. Kirby	Buoyancy: Built-in
Rig: Bermudan	Builders: French Bros (Battlebridge) Ltd.
	Distributors: Stebbings (Burnham) Ltd.

Mr Kirby has the pleasure of seeing his design firmly established as a racing and cruising class of considerable strength. Like any thoroughbred the Wineglass is docile in addition to being a formidable performer and was the first sailing dinghy to be designed for construction in glass fibre. Some of the earlier attempts in this field were merely rehashes of wooden hull designs.

The name derives from the Wineglass section which is considered to be the ideal body shape for deep keel yachts and the Wineglass hull design is based on this principle.

The hull weighs about 260 lb. and the cost is about £300 complete with sails.

Clinker-built Dinghies

Chiefly because of the high cost of manpower, professionally built clinker boats are few. The amateur builder cannot always attain the skills entailed and usually settles for one of the many plywood craft. The traditional methods are far from dying and some examples are reviewed in order of size.

National 12-ft Dinghy

Overall length : 12′   Beam : 4′ 7″
Waterline length : 12′   Sail area : 90 sq. ft
Designers : Several   Buoyancy : Built-in and air-bag
Rig : Bermudan   Builders : Several

Some 2,000 of the class are now sailing, and because it is restricted and not one-design it has been under continuous development since 1935. Because of the relatively small size experimenting in design is not expensive and the 12 ft will always attract the helmsman who is keen to try out new ideas.

The weight of the boat is about 230 lb. and the cost is about £260 complete with sails.

'Yachting World' 14-ft Dayboat

Overall length: 14'	Beam: 5' 7"
Waterline length: 13' 10"	Sail area: 107 sq. ft
Designer: G. O'Brien Kennedy	Buoyancy: Air-bag
Rig: Bermudan or gunter	Builders: Several

The majority of the craft sponsored by the *Yachting World* are breakaways from traditional building methods: the 14-ft Dayboat recognizes that there will always be a demand for the traditional. With some hundreds in existence and a steady annual increase, this dinghy is a sturdy sea boat and is the adopted racing class of a dozen clubs.

The weight of the boat is about 450 lb. and the cost is about £320 complete with sails. It may also be carvel-built.

National 14-ft Merlin Rocket

Overall length: 14'	Beam: 4' 8"
Waterline length: 14'	Sail area: 110 sq. ft
Designers: Several	Buoyancy: Air-bag
Rig: Bermudan	Builders: Several

This restricted design was evolved from the marriage of two smilar types and considerable latitude is left for experimentation. The class is widely raced on both inland waters and estuaries.

The weight of the boat is about 270 lb. and the cost is about £275 complete with sails.

International 14-ft Dinghy

Overall length: 14'	Beam: 4' 8"
Waterline length: 14'	Sail area: 125 sq. ft
Designer: Several	Buoyancy: Built-in and air-bag
Rig: Bermudan	Builders: Several

I include this design among the clinker-built boats because this was the original form. The class rules are restricted and the widest latitude exists for experiment. Hulls are produced in hot- or cold-moulded form, carvel built and even as a hard-chine plywood boat. Now a highly developed racing machine, the International Fourteen is the ancestor of the modern drop-keel sailing dinghy.

Carvel-built Dinghies

When applied to dinghy construction the man-hours involved in laying edge to edge planking has almost extinguished the principle for new building. Except for specialist craft where expense is not spared it is uneconomic to build the smaller sailing dinghies in carvel. The resultant hull is a joy to the eye and touch, very strong and tight as a bottle.

Some very good classes sail round the British coasts, lamentably small in numbers and dwindling year by year. The *Yachting World* 14-ft Dayboat may be carvel built and no doubt there are some examples. I have never seen one, to my regret. Something of a handful for an amateur to build, professional prices would be beyond reasonable reach.

For these reasons I do not attempt to review the classes.

Keel Boats (Daysailers)

National Flying Fifteen

Overall length: 20′	Beam: 5′
Waterline length: 15′	Draught: 2′ 6″
Designer: Uffa Fox	Sail area: 150 sq. ft
Rig: Bermudan	Builders: Several

A strict one-design using the same sail area as the International Fourteen Foot Dinghy, the Flying Fifteen has been built in hot- and cold-moulded wood, plywood, glass fibre, aluminium alloy and even in tufnol. Being inherently stable it appeals to the racing dinghy helmsman who begins to feel

his years, but is not beyond the capabilities of beginners who
have had some experience.

The cost varies with the type of construction and a fair
average is about £750 complete with sails.

'X' One Design

Overall length: 20' 8"	Beam: 6'
Waterline length: 17' 9"	Draught: 2' 9"
Designer: A. Westmacott	Sail area: 210 sq. ft
Rig: Bermudan sloop	Builders: Several

Principally seen in the south, the 'X' One Design is an
example of a veteran class of carvel construction which continues to grow in numbers and there is much keen racing.

Sailing Cruisers

Atalanta

Overall length: 26'	Beam: 7' 9"
Waterline length: 25'	Draught: 18" or 5' 9" with keels lowered
Designer: Uffa Fox	Sail area: 270 sq. ft
Rig: Bermudan sloop	Builders: Fairey Marine Ltd.

The design bristles with innovations: the hot-moulded
hull form clearly shows the influence of years of successful
dinghy production and handling is light and positive. Six
berths are provided and mounted on the specially designed
launching trailer the boat may be used as a caravan whilst on
the road between cruising grounds. One owner has cruised as
far as the Canaries from Southampton.

The basic cost of the boat varies with the type of auxiliary
engine and fittings: it ranges from about £3,900.

Cinder

Overall length: 21' 6"	Beam: 7'
Waterline length: 18'	Draught 3' 3"

Designer: John Westall   Sail area: 129 sq. ft
Rig: Bermudan sloop   Builders: M. F. Sales (Luton) Ltd.
                         South Coast Represenative:
                           Coastal Courses Ltd.

Moulded in glass fibre, this four-berth cruiser is very much in the modern idiom. The equipment is very complete and the price includes the sails and auxiliary engine. £1,500.

Debutante

Overall length: 21′   Beam: 7′
Waterline length: 16′   Draught: 2′ 3″
Designer: Robert   Sail area: 155 sq. ft
           Tucker   Builders: C. S. Blanks Ltd.
Rig: Bermudan sloop   South Coast Representative:
                           Coastal Courses Ltd.

Robert Tucker has distinguished himself by designing a large family of twin-bilge keeled yachts and the Debutante was the first in which he attempted to meet the Junior Offshore Group self-righting requirement. He did so very successfully and has produced a lightweight boat with the maximum of space below at a modest price. The sail area is relatively small and the performance is consequently within the powers of a novice.

Inherent in the twin-bilge keel design is the useful ability of the boat for sitting upright on taking ground.

The cost is about £880.

Escapade

Overall length: 25′ 9″   Beam: 7′ 3″
Waterline length: 21′   Draught: 4′ 3″
Designer: Robert   Sail area: 219 sq. ft
           Tucker
Rig: Bermudan cutter   Builders: C. S. Blanks Ltd.
                          South Coast Representative:
                          Coastal Courses Ltd.

A thicker skin, more ballast, deeper draught and finer lines give the Escapade a better performance than the Debutante, which it resembles in some respects. The cutter rig is flexible enough in balance to permit of sailing to windward under either jib or staysail with the mainsail, or under all three. Nearly 5 ft longer than the Debutante, there is considerably more space below and the self-draining cockpit is reasonably roomy.

The ½-in. skin, generally more substantial build, larger size, and the cutter rig bring the cost of the Escapade up to £1,450 as against £880 for the Debutante.

Folkboat

Overall length: 25' 2"	Beam: 7' 4"
Waterline length: 19' 6"	Draught: 3' 10"
Designer: Association of Swedish Yacht Clubs	Sail area: 250 sq. ft
Rig: Bermudan sloop	Builders: Several

Designed as a clinker hull in 1936, the Folkboat brought sailing within reach of many hundreds of Scandinavians of modest means, as implied by the class name. Now costing on average £2,100, the class grows yearly and hulls are of clinker, cold-moulded or glass fibre construction. A splendid sea boat with several Atlantic crossings recorded – even one to New Zealand – the Folkboat handles easily and has been for many helmsmen the logical step upwards from dinghy sailing.

Gallant

Overall length: 23' 6"	Beam: 7'
Waterline length: 17'	Draught: 2' 9"
Designer: Robert Tucker	Sail area: 180 sq. ft
Rig: Bermudan sloop	Builders: C. S. Blanks Ltd.
	South Coast Representative: Coastal Courses Ltd.

Bigger and tougher sister to the Debutante, the four-berth Gallant is roomier and faster. A simple rig and sturdy fittings make her a good boat for a graduate from dinghy sailing. £980 (less engine).

Selbourne (formerly *Commando*)

Overall length: 28'	Beam: 8' 3"
Waterline length: 20' 6"	Draught: 3' 6"
Designers: Illingworth	Sail area: 266 sq. ft
& Primrose	Builders: M. F. Sales (Luton) Ltd.
Rig: Bermudan sloop	South Coast Representative:
	Coastal Courses Ltd.

If you commission a design from a partnership which has produced so many distinguished ocean-racers a family resemblance is bound to show, even in a fifty-fifty motor-sailer. On looking at the lines of the Selbourne she appears to have more of the characteristics of a purely auxiliary yacht but tucked away below is a Penta diesel engine which takes her along at a good six knots for as long as you like to keep it going.

The layout of the glass fibre hull provides a separate cabin abaft the well and the horses provided for both mainsail and staysail make tacking to windward a simple affair. The cost is about £2,550 inclusive.

Silhouette II

Overall length: 17' 3"	Beam: 6' 7"
Waterline length: 14'	Draught: 1' 8"
Designer: Robert	Sail area: 115 sq. ft
Tucker	
Rig: Bermudan sloop	Builders: A. G. Hurley (Marine) Ltd.

With a sail area less than that of many smaller and lighter dinghies the performance of the Silhouette is not exciting, but it is not meant to be. 1,500 owners in five years is claimed for this shallow-draught cruising boat and much ingenuity is displayed in the layout below to make use of every inch of space. Whilst the standard accommodation provides two berths an alternative arrangement will sleep three.

Costing about £450 (wood), about £550 in glass fibre, a not unusual comment is: 'I don't know how they can do it for the price.' Nor do I: but mass-production methods and a snow-balling demand partly answer the question.

Cruising Catamarans

The great appeal of the twin-hulled craft is in the roomy accommodation below and the abundant space on deck, and in some of the earlier designs these considerations swamped the sailing qualities. Given the combination of shallow-draught hulls, light weight and a good sail plan the catamaran is exciting to sail. If comfortable living can be added to ex-hilarating and safe sailing, the multihull boat may be the answer for many families.

There seems to be a limit to the practical size of the larger catamarans because of the tremendous strains imposed on the bridge joining the two hulls, but research and development may solve the problem. Now under construction is a twin-hulled yacht of 76-ft waterline length and 24-ft beam, ketch-rigged: the designers and builders are the Prout firm which has built so many successful catamarans. In America an even larger vessel is on the stocks.

One large catamaran in which the structural problems seem to have been overcome is James Wharram's *Rongo*, which the designer sailed 10,000 miles in 13 months. She was the first and only catamaran to cross the north Atlantic and the 52-ft hulls (total beam 23 ft) took a tremendous hammering in many gales. Wharram is more interested in development than commercial building at present but one hopes to see him getting into construction.

Perhaps the early problems are now finally solved and we shall see catamarans of even larger sizes than those reviewed, which are among those which have established reputations for their sailing qualities and ease of handling.

Prout 19-ft Cabin Catamaran

Overall length: 19′   Beam: 9′
Waterline length: 17′ 9″   Draught: 11″ (2′ 9″ centreboards
Designer: G. Prout &   down)
        Sons Ltd.   Sail area: 220 sq. ft
Rig: Bermudan sloop   Builders: G. Prout & Sons Ltd.

The first Prout catamarans were no more than two canvas canoe hulls lashed to spars serving as the bridge and from these beginnings sprang the whole family of twin-hulled vessels which bear their name. After the success of the smaller craft several larger cruising prototypes were built with a view to serious production after trials, and the smallest of the standardized range is the 19-ft.

The boat handles very similarly to the Shearwater without being so fast: a lifting cabin top with canvas sides provides reasonable headroom below and the general standard of comfort is higher than could be expected in a single-hulled sailing cruiser costing the same figure of about £950.

Prout 37-ft Cruising Catamaran

Overall length: 37′   Beam: 16′ 3″
Waterline length: 34′   Draught: 12″ (4′ 8″ centreboards
                                 down)
Designers: G. Prout &   Sail area: 923 sq. ft
        Sons Ltd.   Builders: G. Prout & Sons Ltd.
Rig: Bermudan cutter

Before settling on the 37-ft as a standard production Prouts had built several large and successful designs, usually to the special requirements of the owners. One example is *Snow Goose*, built for Mr D. R. Roberts, which has reached a speed of 17 knots: sailing with the fleet (catamarans were not eligible for entry in 1960) in the annual Round the Island Race from Cowes, *Snow Goose* recorded a time which remains unbeaten by any yacht of any size.

From these craft the standard 37-ft catamaran was developed, the hulls having more freeboard to expand the space below decks, naturally at a small sacrifice of speed. *Snow Goose* was designed for weekend cruising, whereas the standard 37-ft caters for fairly prolonged cruising.

Sleeping eight, this cruising catamaran costs about £5,400.

CHAPTER 9

BUYING A BOAT

New or Secondhand? – Inspecting a Secondhand Boat – Surveys – Equipment – Bosun's Stores – Emergency Equipment – Title of Ownership – Insurance – First Sail

Mr PUNCH once offered some advice to those about to marry: 'Don't.'

Something of the kind applies to those about to buy a boat: don't be in a hurry. Take matters in their proper order: decide on your eventual base, learn to handle a boat, mix with others more experienced and get in a season as crew if you can. Most clubs display a list of owners who need a crew and of other members who want to do some crewing. Between the two lists it is not as a rule difficult to get in some sailing time in which you will gain invaluable experience.

It can only lead to disaster if you decide – as did an acquaintance of mine – to have a cruising boat built, take a few days of instruction and then leave for the Mediterranean. Having a smattering of navigation from a book he got no farther than a dozen miles from his home port before going on the rocks.

Throughout this book I have urged you to start in a sailing dinghy, whatever your eventual ambition: let us suppose that you follow this course and decide upon buying a new boat.

Most probably you will have become a regular buyer of the magazines which advertise new and used craft. The principal publications are listed alphabetically:

Light Craft, 2s. 6d.; *Motor Boat & Yachting* (fortnightly), 3s.; *Practical Boat Owner*, 3s. 6d.; *The Yachtsman*, 3s.; *Yachting & Boating Weekly*, 1s.; *Yachting Monthly*, 3s.; *Yachting World*, 3s. 6d.; *Yachts & Yachting* (fortnightly), 2s. 6d.

You will by now have narrowed down your choice of types to one or two and because most new owners will aim at starting in the spring you will probably plan a visit to the International Boat Show in London. Here you will find examples of the type you have decided upon and a crop of new designs as well which can unsettle you in your choice.

Every year sees the optimistic unveiling of several new dinghies. These are usually of good design and workmanship, but go again the following year and see how many have survived. Mostly they disappear.

When buying a boat the eventual secondhand value must be considered. There was a time when new makes of car sprang up like mushrooms and today the established builders can be counted on the fingers. So it is with boats except that most types are produced by a number of builders. The depreciation rate of a well-built and popular type of boat is not to be compared with that of a car. Some larger yachts actually fetch more than their original cost.

I wrote earlier of the many strictly local classes built before and just after the Second World War. Some of these – a good example is the 'X' Class One Design – established a hold outside their home ports and continue to flourish, but many have only a local appeal in a shrinking secondhand market. In the minds of the younger people coming into sailing half a dozen clinker-built boats do not constitute a class. Many of them will want to be sure of getting some racing against helmsmen of their chosen class wherever they may take their boats.

Great difficulties face the producer of a brand-new type, however good the design. If it is to be an economic proposition a large production is essential. It must be accepted nationally rather than locally. Clubs must be induced to adopt the new class and unless it fills an obvious need they will not do so. All the newer designs which have established themselves over recent years have done so because they have met a need.

This means that your choice of a new boat is partly dictated by the adoption of a class by your sailing club and partly by overall popularity. The established classes are numbered in hundreds, some in thousands. Do not be led astray by the high sail number displayed on an exhibit of a new design. It may mean nothing.

Most types are produced by several builders, some of whom are better craftsmen than others. Where a builder has commissioned a design and licenses others to provide similar boats, you can take it that all will make an equally good craft. Obviously it is impossible to list the firms which build the best-class boats and this is another reason why you should not rush into purchase too soon. It will not take long for you to discover in conversation with other sailing men which firms are in good repute.

For preference buy a boat from a builder who is a member of the Ship and Boat Builders' National Federation. This will ensure that some rigid standards have been met and that your boat will be exactly as the designer meant it to be.

Do not judge a boat solely upon the cost, for you will find the same class offered by several builders at differing prices. Have a look under the side decks, run your hand under parts which are out of sight and you will get the impression that many of the cheap examples have been built with an axe. Good fittings and a good finish are expensive but far cheaper in the long run.

All class boats and their sails have to conform to certain measurements, which are verified and certificated by an official authorized by either the Royal Yachting Association or a sailing club. You should always insist that a measurement certificate is supplied with the boat or make the purchase subject to measurement being passed. Without this you may become the owner of a pleasant enough boat but because it does not measure you may well drop a considerable sum when it comes to reselling.

Should you decide that it must be a secondhand dinghy for you, by all means buy a sound example of a local class, if you can do so at such a price that you can afford to give it away when you have done with it. Otherwise buy a boat in an established class, some of which are listed:

Albacore	Shark Catamaran
Alpha	Shearwater Catamaran
Bosun	*Sunday Times* SigneT
Cougar Catamaran	Swift Catamaran
Fairey Falcon Daysailer	Thai Mk.4 Catamaran
Fireball	Wayfarer
Graduate	Wineglass
Gull	*Yachting World* Cadet
Kestrel	*Yachting World* G.P.14
Leader	*Yachting World* Heron
National Enterprise	*Yachting World* Solo
National Firefly	*Yachting World* Catamaran
National Hornet	*Yachting World* Vagabond
National 12-ft	Zenith
National Jollyboat	

There are some obvious omissions from this brief list because the craft concerned are less suitable for beginners. A high performance racing machine must emphatically not be your first boat.

See what is on offer in your selected class in your chosen sailing locality. Club notice boards display advertisements and a few inquiries should help you to decide whether to negotiate a price subject to inspection and approval. Early on you must check up on the measurement certificate and this will particularly apply to boats assembled from kits. Some of these are built with such loving care that they better those produced professionally; some others are terrible.

This is where you are going to need some advice. You will have gathered what others think of your prospective buy from the racing and general reputation standpoints. Ask a professional surveyor to look it over and he is bound to charge a stiffish fee; moreover he has probably had nothing to do with dinghies for years. Your club probably has an appointed Class Measurer and he or some other helpful fellow member should be able to advise you.

If you are driven to use your own resources adopt the following procedure in inspecting the boat, which must always be hauled up ashore:

1. Remove all loose parts – floor-boards, rudder and tiller, oars, boom, etc. Lay the sails out flat.

2. Examine the bottom and sides of the boat for cracks and signs of previous repairs. These should not have weakened the structure if properly executed, but your caution will grow if you discover them instead of the seller pointing them out to you.

3. Check that the rudder, tiller and oars or paddles are sound.

4. Examine the standing rigging for signs of fraying or excessive rusting. Check that the rigging screws will move freely: if they are not stainless steel and have not been well greased when fitting out, they may have rusted solid.

5. Go over halyards and sheets carefully for signs of wear or fraying.

6. Check that the transom fittings are firmly screwed home and examine them closely for signs of undue wear and incipient fracture.

7. Examine the chain plates, transom fittings and horse to see that they are all securely screwed to the boat.

8. Turn the boat over and probe gently with a knife-point for signs of softness at keel, hog, garboard, stem and stempost. This particularly applies to craft of clinker or carvel build.

9. Check the sails for tears and see that the batten pockets are sewn down. Stitching often comes undone here. See that there is no undue wear along the luff of the mainsail, particularly at the head. Check that the wire luffs of foresails are not frayed and that the hanks are free to work. Cotton sails should be closely examined for signs of mildew. If they are sound it will need considerable pressure to pierce them with the point of a needle: easy piercing indicates a short life ahead.

The materials used in construction have a considerable bearing on the useful life of a boat. Most commonly used in the modern dinghies is plywood supplied in flat sheets and the best is that conforming with British Standards Specifications (B.S.S. 1088).

Some builders use imported plywoods which have not been submitted for British Standards Specifications, but which measure up to those obtaining in the country of origin. These are completely satisfactory – I have had many boats built in these plywoods – and it may be assumed that no boat builder of standing will use other than marine plywoods.

Hot-moulded hulls are built only by firms of international standing and repute, cold-moulded by a greater number, and some inquiry into the origin of the latter will help you.

Fastenings are all important and any metal which may corrode and part must be suspect. Copper, bronze, monel or stainless steel are sound, but beware of brass or iron.

If you have found a dinghy of an older type in good condition, the timber and planking material is of importance. You will do well to remember that there was an acute shortage of sound woods in the immediate post-war years and some builders were obliged to use whatever came to hand.

Some details of timbers and planking which you may encounter follow:

Oregon and Columbian Pine. Unless well cared for with adequate paint protection there is a possibility of rotting.

Spruce. A reasonably priced, rather soft wood much used for planking and spars. The grain should be straight and even in texture.

Larch. Less used today than formerly; a wood with a long life.

African Mahogany. Now in wide use, some of the varieties imported in the immediate post-war years proved to be brittle. No boat built within the last ten years should incorporate any suspect wood.

Teak. Heavy but lasts for ever. Very expensive and rarely encountered. But an all-teak boat will see you out – and your grandchildren.

Pitchpine. Still in short supply and an excellent material.

Wych Elm. Perfectly sound for use in salt water but prone to rotting in fresh water.

If a metal or fibreglass hull is being considered the general reputation of the original builder has much importance. In the case of fibreglass, surface crazing or starring usually means that a filling medium has been used and you will be wise to reject it. Probably it is best to seek some expert advice, even in respect of a dinghy, where other than wooden hulls may be bought.

Circumstances may oblige you to buy a keel boat as your first craft. If at all possible you will want a new boat and your general approach should be along the same lines as in buying a dinghy. There is always a good second-hand market for popular and well-established types. Most of these you will find on display at the International Boat Show.

There is a tendency to design small keel boats round the formula of the most berths for the lowest price and this inevitably leads to a cutting down of cockpit space. You will have to visualize where you are going to put the occupants of the berths whilst you are under way and what it is going to be like to cook for six in a very cramped cabin space. Often this formula leads to designs which have negligible sailing qualities and a close resemblance to a caravan with a mast.

If you must consider buying a keel boat let it be no larger than 5 tons (Thames measurement). Between $2\frac{1}{2}$ and 4 tons you will be able to sleep two, and a 5-tonner will give you three berths. Any boat which gives you standing headroom within these limits will almost inevitably mean that it has excessive freeboard and therefore will be a poor performer to windward. The only exceptions will be 'fifty-fifties' – motor-sailers which really rely upon engine power to take them to windward and sail on the easier points.

A new keel boat from the drawing board of a leading designer will always command a good second-hand price, whether one or one hundred have been built.

If you decide to buy a second-hand keel boat you must have

it surveyed. Before you make an offer, which must always be 'subject to survey', you should have been able to estimate the probable value from a study of the advertised prices of similar craft. You will be wise to have a good look over the boat and note any obvious signs of damage or deterioration. Some careful owners have an annual survey and will gladly produce the report along with evidence that work recommended has been done: but this will seldom apply to vessels in the lower price ranges.

Whether the surveyor's report is favourable or not, his services will cost you a fee. Also chargeable to you are hauling-out costs and the repair of anything damaged by the surveyor in the course of inspection. One zealous surveyor I know punched a hole in the side of a steel hull when he was chipping away at a rusted plate to examine the surface. The boat sank and the tentative buyer had to have it raised and repaired. So you must be careful and particularly beware the boat that is offered well below the market average.

Marine insurance brokers can usually supply particulars of local surveyors. If you choose one who has to make a journey for the survey you will have to pay his expenses. The surveyor may need to have panelling removed and keel bolts drawn for examination and this work will be done by the yard which hauls out the yacht. The charges for this should be agreed in advance.

On the whole I have a preference for surveyors who are not also yacht brokers. The disinterested specialist is usually the best. If possible pick on a surveyor who has a reputation for being tough.

Given a favourable survey you can now complete the purchase: you will have paid 10 per cent along with your offer. The report will also be needed for insurance purposes or should you be buying on mortgage or hire purchase.

Should the surveyor recommend that certain work or replacement of gear must be effected you will be quite in order in suggesting a corresponding lowering of the price. If he reports against it, reject the boat at any price. I know of a craft offered in perfect good faith by an owner for £6,000 – it had cost £8,000. Unsuspected dry rot was disclosed on survey and it eventually sold for £700; it was probably dear at that.

Whether you buy new or second-hand the best time of year to purchase is in the autumn, certainly before the New Year if it can be managed. Faced with the costs of winter storage and a spring overhaul the owner of a second-hand boat will be susceptible to an offer. New boats always seem to creep up in price as the new season comes into view.

Equipment

At the International Boat Show during the winter and at any season in the chandler's stores can be seen the collectors of gadgets and gear. With glazed eyes they wander from counter to counter, buying everything from underwater flashlights to shark-repelling fluids. Equipment can be overdone, but there is an essential minimum.

A good stainless steel knife with a locking marlin-spike should be slung round the neck or attached to a belt by a lanyard. Cork-handled sheath knives look very romantic but tend to get in the way in a small boat.

Even a dinghy which is only away from its base for a few hours needs to carry an anchor and at least sixty feet of warp, a bailer or pump and a plastic bucket.

The type of anchor to be used varies with the local type of holding ground: some are good in sand or shingle and useless in mud. The old-fashioned fisherman anchor is as good as any for all-round use even though the stock has to be set up each time it is used.

Soft rubber bailers do not mark paint or varnish in use and a useful type is made in soft plastic, shaped rather like a dustpan. Bailers should always be secured to the boat by a lanyard: one which floats away in a capsize is of little use.

The Wykeham-Martin pump is the type most used in dinghies but care must be taken not to bend the flexible wire piston rod at an acute angle. Once one strand is broken the remainder soon follow and spare wires are not available.

The plastic bucket is useful for carrying odds and ends if hung from a hook under the foredeck.

Some elementary bosun's stores should be aboard. Wrap and seal these items in a plastic bag in case they find their way into the bilge:

> Spare shackles
> Whipping twine
> Beeswax
> Hambro line
> Cotton waste
> Clevis pins and safety-pins
> Adjustable spanner
> Pliers
> Screwdriver

In a cruising yacht the inventory of gear becomes much more comprehensive and a typical list would additionally include:

Main (bower) anchor
200 ft of inch galvanized chain
Kedge anchor and Sea anchor
200 ft of warp
Navigation and riding lights
Compass
Patent log
Fend-offs and bow fender
Foghorn
Boathook
Lead line
Personal buoyancy for each member of the crew
Two or more safety harness sets
Small first-aid kit
At least two good waterproof flashlights and spare batteries.

The bosun's locker really is a locker in the larger yacht and to the simple stores carried in a dinghy must be added:

Spare block
A coil of rigging wire
A complete set of tools (but see that they cannot rust)

A bosun's chair
Spare cordage

The wives of sailing men complain bitterly about the salvage of odds and ends for the bosun's locker that may 'come in handy later on', and it is surprising how often this hoarding is justified.

A cruising yacht should also carry some stores which are not used except in emergency. These must include flares in a sealed package – the function of each is clearly described – an emergency fresh water supply separate from that in everyday use and sealed food supplies. Self-heating soups and stews can be useful but are not always easy to buy. A yacht can go through a hammering storm at sea only to have the crew fail because food supplies are sodden and uneatable.

Title of Ownership

Where sailing dinghies are concerned no particular document is used to prove the title of the new owner. It will be as well to draw up a form of receipt, to be signed by the seller over a sixpenny stamp, which certifies that the vessel is clear of all charges.

Larger vessels can be dealt with in the same way unless they are listed on the British Register of Merchant Shipping. In this are recorded details of any liabilities carried by the yacht and transfers of ownership: there can never be any question as to who is the legal owner of a registered yacht. It is more than probable that your purchase negotiations will be conducted through a broker and he will handle all the details of Register changes. Should the purchase be made direct from the owner an application to the Registrar of Shipping at the port of registration will produce the forms necessary for the transfer.

Insurance

I know of owners who never insure, particularly those whose boats are of low value. It must not be forgotten that a sailing dinghy worth £10 can land the owner with a £25,000 third party claim.

Your best course will be to consult an insurance broker, preferably one close to your sailing base. He will have no particular axe to grind in recommending a suitable policy. He will have a special knowledge of local conditions and can usually get claims settled quickly.

Some companies have specialized in the field of small craft insurance for many years. Many others of high repute in other spheres are beginning to exploit this growing market and you will find some wide variations in premium rates to cover the same risks. The premium paid will be calculated partly on the cruising range proposed, partly on the period in commission and the laid-up period. If the farthest you are likely to go is the Solent, let that be your insured limit. Extra cover for an increased range or for a specific voyage can easily be arranged.

You may think it worth having a reduction in premium by paying an excess of £5 or £10 on each claim. If you are going to race you can get coverage for the attendant extra risks at a slightly higher premium.

Be guided by the broker. Strangely enough, the experience of the policy holder has hardly any influence on the premium rate.

First Sail

Try to contain your impatience to get afloat until you can start off in reasonable wind conditions.

It is to be hoped that you will already have had some experience in the type of boat which you have bought. In this case you will be able to figure out how to get it rigged for launching. All too few builders label the parts of a new boat, and none seem to issue printed instructions on putting the parts together.

If your boat is second-hand the former owner should be able to help you.

Having got afloat see if any leaks are evident. Do not be

FIGURE 26

Boat	Construction	Suitable for Beginner's first boat—A After some experience—B After considerable experience—C Expert helmsmen only—D	Suitable for Car-top—A Trailer—B	Normal crew under sail	Normal crew rowing or outboard	Permitted crew for racing
Cadet	Hard-chine plywood	A—Juniors	A	2	N/A	2
Gull	Hard-chine plywood	A	A	2/3	3/4	2
Heron	Hard-chine plywood	A	A	2/3	3/4	2
SigneT	Hard-chine plywood	A	A or B	2/3	3/4	2

Graduate	Hard-chine plywood	B	2/3	N/A	2
Solo	Hard-chine plywood	B	1/2	N/A	1
Vagabond	Hard-chine plywood	A or B	2/3	3/4	2
Enterprise	Hard-chine plywood	B	2/3	3/4	2
G.P.14	Hard-chine plywood	A	3/4	4/5	2
Leader	Hard-chine plywood	B	2/3	4/5	2
Zenith	Hard-chine plywood	B	2/3	N/A	2
Wayfarer	Hard-chine plywood	A	4/5	5/6	2/3
Hornet	Hard-chine plywood or glass-fibre	B	2/3	N/A	2
Fireball	Hard-chine plywood	A or B	2/3	N/A	2
Firefly	Hot-moulded	B	2	N/A	2
Albacore	Hot-moulded	A	3/4	4/5	2/3

FIGURE 26 – continued

Boat	Construction	Suitable for Beginner's first boat—A After some experience—B After considerable experience—C Expert helmsmen only—D	Suitable for Car-top—A Trailer—B	Normal crew under sail	Normal crew rowing or outboard	Permitted crew for racing
Falcon	Hot-moulded	A	B	4/5	5/6	3/4
Jollyboat	Hot-moulded	C	B	3/4	N/A	3
Cougar Catamaran	Glass-fibre	C	B	2/3	3/4	2/3
Shark Catamaran	Glass-fibre	D	B	2/3	3/4	2
Shearwater Catamaran	Cold-moulded or Glass-fibre	A	B	3/4	4/5	2/3

		A	A or B	1/4	4	2
Swift Catamaran	Cold-moulded	A		1/4	4	2
Thai Mk. 4 Catamaran	Glass-fibre	C	B	2/4	4	2
Yachting World Catamaran	Cold-moulded or Glass-fibre	B	B	2/4	4	2
Alpha	Glass-fibre	B	B	2	N/A	2
Bosun	Glass-fibre	A	B	3/4	4	2
Kestrel	Glass-fibre	A	B	3/4	4	2
Wineglass	Glass-fibre	A	B	3/4	4/5	2
National 12-ft	Clinker	B	B	2	N/A	2
Yachting World Dayboat	Clinker or carvel	A	B	3/4	4/5	2/3
National Merlin Rocket	Clinker	C	B	2	N/A	2
International 14-ft	Clinker, carvel or cold-moulded	D	B	2	N/A	2

too alarmed if there are some in a clinker- or carvel-built boat. Wood takes up fairly quickly and only if the leaks persist have you any grounds for complaint.

There should be no leak in a plywood hull but water can gain entry if the centreboard bolt is not firmly screwed up against its washers. And don't forget that any drainage bungs must be securely in position in any type of boat; self-bailers not firmly fixed in the 'up' position are another possible source of leaks.

If your sails are new they are unlikely to be made of anything but terylene. The cost is now the same as that of cotton sailcloth and the terylene sail is more efficient, has a longer life and can be stowed, if necessary, whilst still wet.

There is an impression that terylene sails need no particular care in breaking in but this is not so. Whilst they certainly need less than cotton sails, stretching in a breeze of not more than Force 3 is recommended. Do not pull the foot of the mainsail too tautly along the boom or overstretch the luff. After a few outings the sail will come to the limit marks on boom and mast.

The foresail luff can be got up bar-taut from the outset. Try to avoid sailing the boat hard on the wind with new sails. An hour of gentle reaching will help sails to a longer life and a shape that will drive the boat.

If the boat carries excessive weather or lee helm the rigging adjustments described in Chapter 2 must be made.

The different types of boats have been reviewed in Chapter 8. In Fig. 26 I have tabulated dinghies with a brief recommendation of their suitability for helmsmen at the various stages of progress. They are listed in the order in which they are reviewed in Chapter 8. Where N/A (not applicable) is inserted in the column 'Normal crew rowing or outboard' this does not mean that they cannot be pushed along by an outboard motor. It is just one of those things like harnessing a racehorse to a milk-float and not contemplated by the designer.

CHAPTER 10

BUILDING A BOAT

Problems Involved – The Workshop – Basic Tools –
Kit-building – Building from Plans – Suitable Types

THE ancient Briton who paddled a coracle built his own
boat because he had to. You are under no such compul-
sion and unless you are quite sure that you can make a good
job of it, abandon the idea of building your own boat. Without exception the owners of home-built boats always find that
the necessary time has been underestimated.

You must be one of the patient kind, for there are few
short cuts. And you must enjoy the work to which you are
committed. If you have come to hate the sight of the thing
before you launch it, the odds are that the boat will not have
been very well built.

One of the most difficult questions to answer is: 'Could I
build a boat like that?' This is constantly being put to me
and is quite impossible to answer. Only a knowledge of your
own capabilities can tell you. Naturally the firm which is
trying to sell you a kit will encourage you. They have to live,
after all.

A leading producer of small boats estimates that the amateur
builder from a kit takes anything up to 200 per cent of the
time allowed in his works to complete a 16-ft sailing boat.
This could mean 400 man-hours – quite a few weekends and
evenings.

The best course is to look over the plans of the boat you
propose to build. It should not take long for you to decide
whether it is within your capabilities, and whether you
should assemble a kit or build from plans. One design (the
SigneT) features full-size plans which can be stuck to the
plywood and almost literally scissored out like a woman's

dress pattern. One hopes that the idea will spread. In several types some vital parts are drawn to the actual size. By far the easiest boats to build are the plywood chine boats and only a skilled woodworker can make a good job of clinker or carvel building.

From the sailing periodicals you can find the names of the firms which specialize in kits. Many of them are builders of complete craft and their instructions are based on their own day-to-day experience. If you decide to build from a kit remember that the short cuts will already have been found. Any of your own can end badly.

Most of the kit-producing firms also supply partly finished hulls. There is more work to be done than might be imagined but the most difficult parts for an amateur to tackle are completed. For example, the centreboard casing will be built and bedded in, the bulkheads are complete and the seams are a glued and screwed watertight joint.

Kits and partly finished boats are always supplied with all the necessary fastenings, glues, paint and varnish.

If you are building from plans do not attempt to build the mast and boom. You will do better to get these components either complete or semi-finished from one of the specialist suppliers.

There can be no satisfaction to equal that of sailing a boat of your own construction. Consider all the aspects before you embark on the enterprise. Your saving in cost will be about one-third of the price of a completed boat and perhaps this will tilt the balance.

Before plunging into the project read *Complete Amateur Boat Building* (Michael Verney, published by John Murray at 20s.). Most public libraries have it or can get it for you.

If you feel that you lack skill or need a refresher, most education authorities run evening woodworking classes at technical schools. In some of the sea-bordering counties special boat building classes are conducted.

The Workshop

One frequently sees press photographs of boats built in the spare room being lowered into the garden. These say much for the patience of a mother or wife, but a dry and well lighted shed or garage would be better. Try to build a boat in the average house and at the back of your mind there is always the nagging thought that you have promised to be out by such and such a date.

All the odds are on the boat being built in the winter and the workshop must be both warm and well lighted. Power tools can be used and so much the better if there is an electricity supply. The workshop should be about half as long again as the boat to be built and the width should not be less than twice the beam.

A solid bench about 2 ft 6 ins. in height and the same in breadth will be needed. If possible the bench should be as long as the boat to be built and unless it is very heavy it should be fixed to the floor. It will need to be equipped with a steel joiner's vice of suitable size and it will be useful to have some drawers underneath it. Four trestles of a convenient height will be needed.

A level floor is essential and it will be an advantage if roof beams or trusses are strong enough to take a block and tackle to help you in moving or turning the boat over.

Basic Tools

Below is a list of the tools needed for building a small boat from a kit. Their cost is modest but if you can afford it power tools will save some time.

> 6-ft steel tape
> 12-inch square
> Claw hammer
> 2 screwdrivers ($\frac{1}{4}$-inch and $\frac{3}{8}$-inch tips). The length of handle is optional.
> Rat-tail and half-round files
> Block plane

Hacksaw and tenon saw

$\frac{1}{4}$-inch hand-drill and a ratchet-brace, both with sets of drills

$\frac{3}{8}$-inch and 1-inch chisels of good quality

Pincers and pliers or a mole-wrench

A set of six G-cramps

A spirit level

2 bradawls

A block of wood to back sandpaper when rubbing down, sandpaper, marking pencils, paint brushes

A hand-worked grinder for sharpening drills and an oil-stone for planes and chisels

The tool chest will need considerable expansion if larger craft are to be built. At one time building from kits was confined to small boats but designs of up to 30 ft in length may now be built from either kits or plans. The saving in cost may be as much as one-half compared to the one-third saving on a home-built dinghy, and many examples may be seen at any sailing centre. The following additions are needed:

Electric drill

Electric bandsaw, small size

Panel saw

36-ft steel tape

Dividers

Steel jack-plane

Some additional G-cramps

Long screwdriver with $\frac{7}{16}$-inch tip. Some screwdriver brace bits

Rebate and moulding planes

A small set of cold chisels

Compass saw

Some larger chisels and two gouges

A wooden mallet

A set of spanners and an adjustable spanner

Kit-building

If you have decided to build from a kit you cannot go wrong if you buy from one of the specialist firms. All the materials will be of approved marine quality and much care is taken to see that all parts fit together with the minimum of adjustment. Most firms check the transom, bulkhead and centreboard box on a jig, drilling them so as to make a mistake in lining up virtually impossible. In most cases the component parts are clearly stamped.

Your kit will arrive as a flat package including the plans and a detailed instruction book. In some cases it is possible to rent a home-constructor's jig for a nominal monthly sum.

You must first check the contents and claim at once for anything missing from the detailed list of parts. This is most unlikely to be necessary but it will be an exercise in getting to know the parts of your boat at an early stage.

Read through the instruction book. Most of these are very clearly written but if you have a doubt on any point either get advice from another home-builder or write to the supplier, who would far rather clear up any ambiguity than have you make a mess of the job.

Building from Plans

One of the drawings, usually that showing the general arrangement, incorporates a list of materials. Timber suppliers will usually help by cutting to convenient sizes but plywood sheets are supplied only in various stock sizes. In the case of the latter you must always buy an approved marine ply. Glues and metal fastenings must also conform to marine specifications.

The types of fittings to be used are usually specified by name and are obtainable through marine chandlers. You must not expect to find everything waiting in stock against the time when you get round to needing it. Get all the materials ordered at once and into your workshop as soon as possible.

Most probably your home building will be done in the winter. Make a point of ordering your sails (and metal mast, if you are going to use one) for a definite spring delivery date.

FIGURE 27

Boat	Kit or Plans	Address for Information
SigneT	Both available	Hon. Secretary Mr T. A. Field SigneT Class Owners' Association, Merienda, Greenhill, Elton, Peterborough, Northants.
International Cadet	Both available	International Cadet Class Secretary, Dorset House, Stamford Street, London, S.E.1.
Gull	Kit or part completed only	Small Craft Blue Hulls Ltd., Blockley, Gloucestershire.
Heron	Both available	*Yachting World*, Dorset House, Stamford Street, London, S.E.1.
G.P.14	Both available	*Yachting World*, Dorset House, Stamford Street, London, S.E.1.
Vagabond	Both available	*Yachting World*, Dorset House, Stamford Street, London, S.E.1.
Light Craft Graduate	Both available	*Light Craft*, 24 Store Street, London, W.C.1.
Yachting World Solo	Both available	*Yachting World*, Dorset House, Stamford Street, London, S.E.1.
National Enterprise	Both available	Jack Holt Ltd., The Embankment, Putney, London, S.W.15.
Wayfarer	Kit or part completed only	Small Craft Blue Hulls Ltd., Blockley, Gloucestershire.
Fireball	Kit or part completed only	Chippendale Boats Ltd., Lower Quay, Fareham, Hants.

Many an amateur sees precious sailing time slipping away because he forgot to order in time.

Suitable Types

Details of the types listed below are given in Chapter 9 and are arranged in order of simplicity. All are available as partly completed hulls. This does not exclude other designs, of which there are many of great merit: only a limited number can be reviewed in this book.

The keel boats listed below in order of simplicity are not among those reviewed in Chapter 9 but are specifically designed for home building.

One last piece of advice to home builders: measure twice and cut once.

FIGURE 28

Boat	Kit or Plans	Address for Information
Yachting World Rambler	Both available	*Yachting World*, Dorset House, Stamford Street, London, S.E.1.
Yachting World People's Boat	Both available	*Yachting World*, Dorset House, Stamford Street, London, S.E.1.
Yachting Monthly Senior	Plans only	*Yachting Monthly*, 3 Clements Inn, London, W.C.2.
Yachting World Buccaneer	Both available	*Yachting World*, Dorset House, Stamford Street, London, S.E.1.
Yachting World Seahorse	Both available	*Yachting World*, Dorset House, Stamford Street, London, S.E.1.
Yachting Monthly Waterwitch	Plans only	*Yachting Monthly*, 3 Clements Inn, London, W.C.2.

CHAPTER 11

MAINTENANCE

Laying up a Dinghy – Laying up a Keel Boat –
Laying up Glass Fibre Hulls – Sailing Clothes –
The Winter's Work – Glass Fibre Refits

THE old days when yachting was a strictly seasonal diversion for a privileged few are gone for ever, thank goodness. Sailing, do-it-yourself sailing for the most part, has taken its place but a few vestigial traces of the old days remain: the duration of the season, for example.

When a skipper and paid hands normally manned almost any yacht, it came into commission in mid May and laid up again at the end of September in British waters. There was a long winter to get through and when the yacht appeared at the beginning of each summer the paint shone and the varnish sparkled. Under the indulgent eye of the skipper the owner helmed his yacht in a few races because it was the thing to do at that particular time and many must have ended the short season feeling that the skipper had more rights in the vessel than the owner. It was something like the difference between playing football and watching a match on television. Of course there were some exceptional owners who really were in charge – MacMullen, for example, whose *Down Channel* ought to be in every sailing library.

The idea of May to September still lingers on when in fact many owners sail from mid March to the end of October. But at some time a boat has to be laid up, and refitting started. The foundation of this work is laid when you have decided that you really have had the last sail until next spring. You must make a list of the various jobs that you have been meaning to do but have put off because there was no real urgency. Do this whilst they are still fresh in your mind and keep the list in your pocket: you will remember items of new gear that you will want to investigate at the chandlery and all this will be a sort of occupational therapy to help you through the winter.

Laying up a Dinghy

A dry shed of your own giving plenty of space round the boat in which to work is the ideal, but you may have to hire some covered accommodation in a boatyard. In this case you should make sure that the yard is agreeable to allowing owners to do their own work. Not so unreasonable, if you reflect that the undercover space is in use for only about half the year and the returns, including profits on refitting, have to pay for the other half. Most yards co-operate with owners wishing to do their own refitting but it will help all concerned if you decide the exact dates when you wish to get at your boat. Dinghies are usually stored on racks, upside down, and you will not be very popular if you arrive without warning just because it happens to be a fine Saturday morning. Fix your date for starting the refit, and the earlier the better: conditions are chaotic when all the late starters get going together.

Before laying up, the boat must be thoroughly washed down with fresh water, for lingering traces of salt will mop up moisture and make damp patches which may cause difficulties later on. Remove floor boards and any loose parts, the centre-board and bungs or hatch covers of watertight compartments: if there is air-bag buoyancy this should be taken from the boat.

Shrouds and forestay should be removed from the mast, each part being labelled: you may as well examine wires for signs of fraying at once. Bend the wire at successive points and if any strands break it is due for renewal. You will also check the bottle screws for signs of excessive play in the thread or any incipient fractures, making notes of the replacements as you go.

Remove the halyards from the mast, not forgetting to tie a piece of twine to the end of each tail so that you can pull the halyard back again. Fail to do this and you may have ahead of you hours of time wasted in fishing about with wire pushed down inside the top of the mast to the sheaves at the foot. Examine the wire of each halyard, the eye which receives the shackle and the splice between the rope tail and the wire itself. Label each and make a note of any replacement.

All metal and wire parts which will be serviceable for next season should be protected with vaseline or lanoline but take care that rope is untouched by either.

Examine rudder and transom fittings for signs of play or wear: they undergo large strains and it may be as well to replace any doubtful screws.

Examine the toestraps and their fastenings very closely and if there is a sign of wear they must be scheduled for replacement. Toestraps have a hard life and their failure can tip you ungracefully over the side. Canvas webbing is cheaper but cannot be relied upon for more than one season. Terylene seems to last for ever and is far cheaper in the long run.

Go over sheets carefully and if there are signs that they are wearing out schedule them for replacement. A mainsheet may sometimes be given a new lease of life by reversing it if the wear is not excessive but be ruthless in replacement if there is any doubt. Wash all the serviceable sheets in warm fresh water to remove the salt.

By now your list will be fairly formidable and you may as well complete the job by estimating the amounts of paint and varnish you will need. You will feel full of virtue if you put all the new gear and paint on order at once for a forward date.

If you are storing with a yard which will also do the refitting get the details in as early as possible. Many yards need work in the early winter and will sometimes give a worthwhile discount to secure it.

If your dinghy must be stored in the open she will come to no harm under a good canvas or plastic cover raised from the deck to allow air to circulate freely, hatch-covers and bungs of watertight compartments being removed or eased to allow them to 'breathe'. The keel should be laid on timbers which take the weight equally and chocks put under the bilges to support the boat. The mast should be under cover if possible, but if it has to remain in the open it must be evenly supported, to avoid any danger of warping, and clear of the ground. The groove which receives the mainsail luffrope must be laid undermost.

Take the sails home with you, spread them out in a dry place and go over them very thoroughly. Wear usually shows at head-board, stitching of seams, batten-pockets and cringles, and any repairs should be made at once. Small holes may be darned, larger ones may need patches of the same material, and never use cotton thread for repairing terylene sails or vice versa. The luffwires of foresails should be bent to detect through the sailcloth any signs of fraying and sent to a sail-maker for replacement if necessary. Any repairs which you judge to be beyond your capacity should be dealt with by a sailmaker and as early as possible. By early December most lofts are so full of work for the new season that repairs brought in later cannot be accepted.

All repairs should be done before the sails are washed and this can often be done in a domestic washing machine. The alternative is to put them in a bath in a mild detergent – some special varieties are stocked by most chandlers – and wash them thoroughly. This is a quite formidable job for large sails and I know many owners who say that the only solution is to get in the bath oneself. Many laundries in sailing centres make a good job of washing sails at a reasonable charge and will certainly do it better than the average owner. Sailmakers will also arrange for this to be done.

Once clean, sails should be put away in a dry place, loosely rolled. Terylene must not be ironed (if you are that much of a perfectionist), for this may damage the hot-rolled finish which makes the fabric impervious to wind.

Wooden battens can be rubbed down and given a coat of varnish when you are dealing with the hull.

Have a look at the seizings of foresail hanks when the sail

has been washed, and replace any doubtful, securing with waxed twine. Piston hanks can be treated with a minute quantity of penetrating oil.

Laying up a Keel Boat

The costs of laying up a keel boat mount annually and if you elect to do so under cover you may be faced with some problems: this sort of problem, for example, which confronted one of my friends.

His seven-tonner was hauled up by a large yard most efficiently and the refitting schedule for the spring had been the subject of estimate and acceptance. Having some spare time he drove down on a sunny winter day with the idea of installing some oddments of deck gear he had bought, generally pottering round and thinking of the next season. He had hardly drilled the first hole in a hatch-coaming before a shop-steward popped a head over the side demanding to see his union card. My friend had to abandon his happy pottering, of course; the new fittings went on in the spring when he was afloat on his mooring and nobody was better off in the long run.

If you aim to do any refitting yourself you must make quite sure with the management what limits there are: some yards stipulate that they shall do all work on the outside of the hull, leaving owners free to work below. If you find a yard which can agree to the complete refit being done by the owner it is only fair that you should lodge with it your order for supplies.

Laying up in a shipyard entails fixing a date coinciding with a suitable tide; the unstepping, stripping and storage of the mast must also be arranged. This should be fixed well in advance, as should the date for the spring relaunching.

As soon as possible after hauling up, go over the gear rigging and sails with the shipyard foreman and give early instructions for renewals.

Probably two-thirds of keel boats in British waters are laid up in the open under covers; since hauling-up by a shipyard is involved this means that you must make the same arrangements as for shed storage. The restrictions on work by the owner are usually lighter but against this you will depend on having dry weather for outside painting and varnishing and these must be complete by the date you have selected for re-launching. You will throw the programme badly out of gear if your boat is not ready when the time comes. Storage in the open costs about half as much as in a shed.

One of the advantages of the light-hulled twin-bilge keel hulls such as the Silhouette or the Debutante is that their light draught allows them to be floated on to special trailers for road transport. Many owners arrange with contractors to have their boats brought to their homes and more than half of a good painting day need not be wasted in driving down to the coast. The transport costs are not light but you will certainly pay less than if you store with a shipyard.

When the boat is hauled up the bottom should at once be cleaned of all barnacles and weed and hosed down generously with fresh water. If there is a water-cooled auxiliary engine the system must be drained, as must fresh water tanks and the W.C. There should always be an engine handbook aboard and you will find in it very clear instructions for the winter care of the auxiliary. Always drain off the petrol left in the tank; water and dirt inevitably get in during the off season. Take home the magneto and have the batteries checked and recharged.

An alternative is to lay up in a mud berth and most ship-yards can offer some facilities. Cheaper than laying-up ashore, you will still have to haul up at some stage to attend to the underwater painting. Some owners try to dispense with this by laying their craft against a convenient quay and painting between tides, but this practice, whilst acceptable for a mid-season repaint, is not recommended. Before deciding on a mud berth you must make inquiries about gribble worm, which attacks underwater surfaces very destructively. A cover should always be fixed over the boat.

Some mud berths are very muddy indeed and it may even be possible only to get aboard when there is enough water to float a dinghy. This is an aspect you must consider before deciding. The normal winter care of the auxiliary engine and drainage of fresh water and W.C. must be remembered.

Mud berths are frequently in isolated places and your cabin doors and all hatches must be properly secured. It is wisest to take home the compass, clock, and anything else which might might appeal to an intruder.

Few owners decide on laying up afloat although to do so has much to commend it if the mooring is in reasonable shelter. Some hulls are likely to open up if they become too dry and may go through the winter better than others stored ashore, particularly those in the open. Eight weeks of cold dry winds last winter wrought havoc.

Laying up afloat is certainly the cheapest winter plan but against it is the fact that you have to go out in a dinghy whenever you want to do some work. And you are almost certain to find you need something which can only be obtained ashore.

You will do well to have your mast unstepped if you decide to lay up afloat and whether you can do this with the help of your crew will depend on the size. Damage to a mast can be expensive and this work is best done by a shipyard.

Wherever you lay up you must remember that your insurers are closely interested. You must see that all particulars are available, remembering that if you lay up early you are due for a small rebate; if you decide that the weather looks like holding for another few tempting weeks, check that your policy holds you covered. Extensions can be arranged for the price of a telephone call and a small extra premium. This is one of the reasons why you will do better to deal with a local insurance broker. Knowing the area, he can advise the insurers as to the safety of your winter arrangements; it won't cost a penny more and may even save money.

Laying up Glass Fibre Hulls

One of the main attractions is that much less maintenance work is involved and some builders have gone to dangerous extremes by advertising that there is absolutely none involved. These claims could lead owners to neglect even the minimal care required.

Storage in the open is perfectly acceptable and the colour will not fade if the hull comes from one of the reputable builders who use the material without the addition of fillers.

Care must be taken to see that the boat is well and evenly supported at a number of points; kinking in the skin may become permanent if this is not carefully arranged, preferably by chocks and shores which bear up against under-skin ribs or stringers.

The hull should be cleaned off externally and internally with fresh water and the normal drainage of any auxiliary engine and fresh water systems should follow.

Small light alloy runabout and dinghy hulls can be laid up in the same way. Should you have become the owner of a steel hull it can be dealt with in the same manner as wooden craft of the same size.

Sailing Clothes

Oilskins, and sailing clothes generally, often get stowed away at the end of a season to be remembered only when spring is not far away. Woollen clothing will be deeply impregnated with salt moisture and may need several washings to clear it, and this is best done at the end of the season. Allegedly showerproof canvas smocks will be stiff and stained with sea water and many of them become limp and thin to the touch when washed; this may be because they are not made of sailcloth, whatever the label states. A thinner cloth thickened up by fillers often substitutes and the canvas feeling disappears with the first wash. Having got them clean, try treating smocks with one of the rainproof finishes which can be had in any good chandlery.

The old type of oilskin has vanished in favour of plastic materials. These need to be sponged in warm water, grease stains being treated with soap. Few plastics will withstand petrol or spirit cleaning and experimentation is not advisable.

Tears and parted seams should be repaired by patches on the inside, always using a suitable adhesive and plastic material. You cannot mend plastic with a tyre repair outfit.

The fastenings of plastic oilskins should be checked: 'poppers' tend to tear away and can be refastened to a backing of plastic material stuck to the inside of the garment. 'Evo-Stick' is a reliable adhesive for this purpose and some manufacturers sell small repair outfits for about half-a-crown. Metal zip-fasteners corrode easily and even the nylon types become encrusted with salt. Wash them in fresh water and rub the teeth with some beeswax; a liberal application seems to ensure easy zipping for a whole season.

Plastic oilskins should be stored on hangers after they have been carefully turned inside out.

Most dinghy sailors now use open mesh plastic sandals which need nothing beyond a wash under a tap before putting away. Rubber-soled canvas shoes will certainly have become salt stained and need washing in fresh water. After drying them in the open stuff them with newspaper and store them.

Ankle-length rubber boots may develop leaks and these can be mended with a tyre repair outfit. All traces of salt water must be eliminated before patching, otherwise moisture will be trapped under the patch and it will come off. Rubber boots should also be stuffed with newspaper before storing.

The Winter's Work

You must make no mistake about it: most of the spring refit must be done in the winter. All too many owners put the boat away when the season peters out, attend the Club laying up dinner and dance and forget all about it for weeks at a time. Quite suddenly the new season comes up with a rush and because you haven't ordered that new sail, the replacement forestay or whatever it is, there you are on the shore and everyone else has gone off for a sail.

As a basis for the winter work you have that list you drew up at the end of last season and it is to be hoped that all the material you will need is on order. Some sort of a programme must be drawn up. If you own a wood hull you must decide how much repainting is necessary: assuming average conditions of use you will need an undercoat and two coats of enamel, and anything up to three coats of varnish on the bright work. Putting on the paint is short work; preparation is what takes the time and pays the dividends.

Having decided how much work is to be done, try to reduce this to a man-hours figure. There is not much to guide you on this – only you know your own capacity for work. As a very rough indication a sixteen-foot dinghy can be prepared and given an undercoat and two coats of enamel on the hull and three coats of varnish on the bright work in about forty professional man-hours. If you double this time and then double it again to allow for going off to buy oddments you have forgotten and for chatting with other owners, you will not be far out. If your boat is housed under cover your programming is easier, but you will be very dependent on good light if your boat is tucked away in a dark corner.

If your boat is stored outside you are absolutely dependent on the weather and if the right day dawns other plans must be abandoned if you want to get sailing at the beginning of the season.

The first thing to be done is to see that the inside of the hull is completely clean and the easiest method is to use a vacuum cleaner to clear out dust and accumulations of sand from last season. If no power is available it must be done the hard way and cleaning out will be necessary after each internal rubbing down.

Unless the colour of the hull is to be changed drastically from a dark shade to something much lighter, a good rubbing down with 'wet and dry' glasspaper will be all that is needed. If a lighter colour is to be used all the old paint will have to be removed down to bare wood, either by burning off or by using a caustic acid stripper. In both cases caution will be necessary: only the paint must be burned by the blowlamp, without scorching of the timber. If caustic acid stripper is used it should be applied in patches of 4/5 sq. ft at a time, using a brush reserved for this purpose alone; no amount of cleaning will enable you to use it for ordinary painting. A few seconds after the stripper has been applied you can set to work with a scraper and remove the paint. Second treatments are sometimes necessary.

Once the paint is removed the hull must be wiped clean of fragments with turpentine substitute, generously so where caustic stripper has been used, for any lingering traces will attack the new paint. From then on the sequence of paint coats follows – primer, undercoat and enamel coats, rubbing down between each coat to provide a key for the paint.

Varnishing requires the most careful preparation: if it has gone badly over an extensive area you may decide to strip it all off and start all over again. The difficulty is to know when to stop, for to do one side of a foredeck shows up the other side.

The average boat displays patches of bare wood from which damp will have crept below the surrounding varnish. After an overall rub down the lifted varnish skin edging the bare patches will show very clearly, and this must be removed until only sound material surrounds the bare patch, which is then given a priming and an ordinary coat to bring it up to the surrounding standard. Once the bare patches have been dealt with the attack on the overall surfaces can begin. By the time you have finished the rubbing down between each coat, the cleaning off and the brushing on, you will be getting heartily sick of the whole thing. But you will glow with virtue.

Between spells of painting you can deal with other items on your list. You must be sure to let each coat harden before applying the next and you will have had a most exceptional weekend if you can get on two coats in two days. Only in dry and warm weather is this feasible.

Paint manufacturers are anxious that you should make the best use of their products and your best course will be to get a booklet of instructions from the maker. Stick to the book and you will not go far wrong.

Polyurethane paints and clear finishes have come along

fast in recent years and there can be no doubt that they are more durable than ordinary paint and varnish. If you decide to use them stick very closely to the instructions, particularly those referring to temperature and humidity.

A vague idea exists among newcomers that power tools can help in the rubbing down work and so they can, used with knowledge. No doubt the image of Superman Do-it-Yourself, who knocks up a stately home with the aid of a basic power unit and a kit of special tools, has been over-emphasized in advertising. A badly handled power sander can damage a hull irreparably. If you do use one, get in some training on domestic paintwork before using it on your boat.

Air-bag buoyancy used in dinghies should be checked for leaks and mended with the appropriate material. Valves must be in working order and when the bags are refastened inside the boat they must be firmly anchored in position or they will be useless in a capsize.

Glass Fibre Refits

If the hull has come through the season without a scratch there is nothing to be done beyond cleaning down and painting or varnishing the small amount of wooden external trim.

Minor scratches can be ignored but spoil the appearance of the boat and are easily rubbed out by 'wet and dry' glasspaper. Some owners use liquid metal polish, which is mildly abrasive, for the purpose. When the scratch is rubbed out finish off with a coat of wax polish.

Deep scratches may be painted out with a matching polyurethane after the surrounding surface has been wet rubbed down to make a key. The snag here is the matching and for this reason many builders in glass fibre supply hulls in any colour you choose so long as it is white. If you have a hull which is through-coloured the constructors may be able to supply resin from which you can make up a matching polyester mix.

If the glass fibre mat is exposed it must be thoroughly cleaned and dried, after which matching resin coats must be

applied to build up the damaged area 'proud' of that surrounding it. The patch can then be filled and rubbed down
so as to leave no trace.

I will repeat these maxims:
   The spring refit begins in the autumn.
   Order supplies and replacements in the autumn.
   Calculate a working programme and double the time you
      first thought of.
   If housed with a shipyard arrange the spring relaunching
      date in the autumn.
   Be ruthless in replacing doubtful gear.

CHAPTER 12

UNDER ENGINE

*Power Boat Types – Handling the Runabout –
Handling larger Power Craft*

Power Boat Types

PERHAPS it is their resemblance to the family car which first attracts so many buyers to the small runabout. A windscreen with wipers, a car-type steering wheel, a gear lever and electric starting all add to the comfortable illusion that driving afloat is not very different from driving on the roads, except that there is far more room. And the awful *mystique* of sailing often enough tips the balance for the man who wants to get some sea air without bothering about sails.

Compared with the cost of a car one gets a lot of boat for the money: towed behind the family saloon it is easy to imagine sunlit weekends on whichever piece of coast takes the fancy. Water-skis for the teenagers, picnics, fishing, maybe: it all seems easy enough, and out comes the cheque book.

The larger cruising boats are fairly expensive and cost anything from £4,000 upwards for four-berth accommodation. There is no question of towing these craft to various centres and moorings or a quayside berth must be located. Many of the most successful designs are based on the motor fishing vessels used off the north-east coasts and because they derive from working craft are generally easier to handle and steadier in a seaway than some of the rather flashy 'gin-palace' types.

The more expensive craft are often diesel powered, more costly initially but cheaper to run because fuel consumption is about half that of petrol and at about half of its price. Some will be twin engined and for this reason easier to handle.

For a given length the beam will be proportionately broader than that of a sailing boat and this makes for more comfortable living conditions below. Engines and fuel tanks will take up a good deal of space but in some designs – the Dell Quay Ranger is a good example – the use of 'inboard-outboard' plant makes much additional room below. Here the engines are of a special type, positioned hard against the transom with a horizontal-vertical-horizontal drive to the propellor, which itself swivels to give very positive steering.

Double-ended lifeboats sold off from liners which are being broken up are often enough converted into cabin cruisers, with varying success. If you contemplate buying such a boat a survey is essential.

The heart of any power boat is in the engine, or engines. A marine motor is exposed to dampness and corrosion which are never met with in a car and for this reason amateur power-plant conversions must be suspect. Many of the great car manufacturing concerns make marine versions of road engines and these are in every way satisfactory.

Cruising power boats fall into two broad categories of hull shapes, round bilged hulls of fairly shallow draught and planing hulls designed to lift in the water at speed. The latter sometimes feature a vee-shaped form forward, flattening off towards the stern. Because behaviour in a seaway attracts me more than high speed I lean towards the round bilge type. Relatively small though it is the keel has a steadying effect against rolling and if a small sail area is added it will do much to help the keel. In a fair wind the sail will also help to take the vessel along or even get you into port in the case of engine failure. A good example of a sound design on those lines is the Fairey Fisherman at a price of about £4,500.

Going back to the smaller runabout types, mostly powered by outboards, the choice is very wide indeed. Many of them are sound boats if they are used for the purpose for which they are designed, on a good day in smooth water. Some of them are horrible, only resembling a boat because they are sharp at one end and blunt at the other, finished off with car-type fins and winkers.

If you decide on a runabout you should buy one from a

reputable builder. If you are able to go to the Boat Show you can get impartial advice from the Advisory Bureau but avoid the boat displayed on a roadside filling station at what seems to you a very low price. In most cases it is there on a sale or return basis and built into it is a hefty motor car rate of discount. It must be added here that many car retailers of high repute have properly staffed retail boat departments and these may be depended upon.

Buoyancy is very seldom built into runabouts and its installation, possibly in the form of air-bags, is a must. If the builder specifies a 20 h.p. outboard don't instal 40 h.p. under the impression that you will go twice as fast. I saw a case of this last year: already weighed down in the stern by a much heavier unit than planned, the hull stood on the transom as soon as the throttle was opened, filled, and sank at once.

Handling the Runabout

You have selected a launching point, the trailer is hitched to the car and the sea is two hours away. On the face of it, all you have to do is drive down, unhitch the trailer, launch your runabout and go.

There is a good deal more to it than this.

You must:

1. Know the Rules of the Road: if you have some idea of what sailing craft are doing you will be able to anticipate their movements and keep clear.
2. Know local rules and by-laws affecting speed limits, water-ski-ing, etc.
3. Know what tidal movements there will be while you are out, otherwise you may find the water level so reduced that the boat cannot be hauled on to the trailer again.
4. Know what weather conditions are forecast.
5. Know the meaning of buoys.
6. Know the layout of shoals or other hazards at the launching point.

Assuming you have planned the excursion round these six

basics, that you have a sufficient supply of clean fuel, paddles or oars to help in an emergency, fire extinguishers and a bailer or pump, you can unhitch your trailer and trundle it to the edge of the water. You and the crew will be wearing your personal buoyancy.

You will obviously avoid the soft spots into which the trailer wheels will sink and the hull is floated off it when there is enough depth of water. It is more than likely that there will be insufficient depth to lower the shaft of the outboard at once and the boat must be rowed or paddled out until there is. Turn the bow in the general direction you want to go and start the engine.

Among moored boats you should move at reduced speed and you must keep very clear of all mooring buoys. A rope strop caught in your propellor will put an abrupt end to your excursion.

Practically all runabouts have planing hulls and this means that they make less wash at higher speeds. Against this there are local speed limit by-laws which will be enforced much more rigorously as time goes on. So that if you reduce speed when you approach sailing craft you may well knock up more of a chop instead of less. I do not know how to advise you, but, off the record, you will probably do better to maintain a reasonable planing speed *and keep well clear*.

You will have a local chart or harbour plan and you should keep within the buoyed limits. There will be no difficulty in steering whilst the engine is going but when approaching a shore it must be stopped before there is any danger of the propellor fouling the bottom. An oar or paddle should be ready for use as a rudder to steer the boat to the shore as way falls off.

Should you run into a heavy head sea the engine speed should be reduced. It may be great fun to smack from wavetop to wavetop in moderation, but if you overdo it the hull may be weakened from the hammering – water can be very hard. Also, when the hull is almost clear of the water in these leaps there is a moment of great instability in which capsize may occur.

In the case of a following sea the boat must be kept trimmed by moving the crew so that the engine does not bury itself.

Any water coming aboard must be bailed or pumped out at once, particularly if you run into heavy weather. In the case of an engine failure in a chop, keep the bow of the boat into the waves with oars or paddles.

At all times keep a lookout for floating driftwood or seaweed: the former can hole the boat and the latter can wrap round the propellor to stop the engine.

Handling Larger Power Craft

I wrote earlier that twin screws eased some handling problems in larger craft but this only applies when they are 'handed' to turn in opposite directions. In the rare cases where they are not, a twin-screw vessel is no easier to handle than a single-screw boat. In the case of a single-screw craft there will be a tendency for it to turn in one direction more readily than in another, and this will govern much of your manoeuvring in a confined space.

Space does not permit a detailed look at all the problems which may arise, but they chiefly centre round turning the boat in a confined space and stopping it when coming up to a mooring or alongside a quay. There must always be an appreciation of the effect of the wind, for the high topsides and relatively shallow draught will cause the boat to be blown to leeward. This drift can be countered by using increased engine power, which is the last thing you want to do in a confined space. A course must be worked out so that whilst still going slowly ahead the boat 'crabs' to the objective.

When way is to be checked reverse drive must be used in good time, for screws have only about half the bite they have in forward drive. As the boat slows you will have to remember that if it begins to make sternway the rudder will become effective, possibly causing you to miss your objective.

Take a simple example.

You are aiming to pick up a mooring buoy fifty yards away on your starboard bow and the wind is blowing from the starboard beam. To offset drift you are going slow ahead, helm over to starboard. Realizing that you are going to over-run the buoy you put the engine to full astern. The boat checks as it nears the buoy and the bow swings exasperatingly to port as sternway begins.

Except for the complications of drift from wind and tide, going astern calls for much the same wheel movements as would be required in backing a car.

Twin screws, provided they are 'handed', simplify the turning manoeuvres because one engine going half ahead and the other full astern will turn your vessel in her own length in slack water and little wind.

There are few problems in leaving a mooring. You will have to see that the rope strop of the buoy does not wrap itself round a propellor and this can be avoided if the boat is moved very slowly ahead, a member of the crew carrying the buoy down to the stern and only putting it overboard as the boat moves clear.

Leaving a quay at which craft are moored ahead and astern of you may not be so easy. Your aim to get the bow out, cast off the last securing rope and get under way may have to take into consideration what the wind and tide are doing. Sometimes it may be necessary to turn her on a spring – pulling against a rope fixed to a stern cleat and passed round a bollard on the quay more or less abreast the bow. It is not, in fact, as easy as you might have supposed.

If you buy or charter a power craft you must get somebody who knows the boat to spend some time showing you how she handles. As soon as possible turn her full circle under engine in both directions so that you have an idea of the amount of sea room needed.

All that I have written applies equally to auxiliary yachts, which come under all the rules applying to power craft as soon as the screw begins to turn.

GLOSSARY

A

Aback. A sail having its clew held or sheeted to windward.

Abaft. Behind.

Abeam. At a right angle to the fore-and-aft line.

Adjustment (*of compass*). The insertion of small iron strips and magnets into a compass to offset local magnetic errors of the needle.

Aft. Towards the stern.

Ahead. Forward, in the direction of the bows.

Alternating light. A light for navigational aid showing different colours alternately.

Amidships. In the middle of a vessel.

Anchor buoy. A marker buoy attached to an anchor to show its position so that vessels may avoid fouling it by anchoring across it.

Anchor light. A white riding light visible for 360° which must be displayed by a vessel at anchor. Whilst dispensed with in quiet creeks it is essential where other craft may be moving at night.

Anti-cyclone. A rotary high-pressure area, usually bringing fine weather.

Anti-fouling. Special paint or composition applied to the bottom of craft lying on moorings to prevent marine growths.

Apparent wind. Difference indicated by a masthead flag as between the true direction of the wind and that created by the movement of a vessel under way.

Armstrong's patent. Hand-operated machinery, winches or capstans.

Athwart. Across a vessel from side to side.

B

Back. Sheeting a sail to windward. An anti-clockwise change in direction of the wind.

Backstay. There are two varieties, both of which brace the mast against oblique pressures. Seldom found on dinghies but common on keel boats.

    1. A wire support running from the stern of the boat to the top of the mast.

    2. Running backstays are adjustable and run from the mast to points abaft of it on either side of the vessel.

Backwinding. Where the slot between foresail leech and the mainsail is too narrow the partial vacuum on the lee side of the mainsail is distorted. The mainsail is then said to be backwinded. (See Chapter 2, p. 43.)

Baggywrinkle. Padding, usually made of yarn, attached to shrouds to prevent chafing of sails and running gear. Now seldom seen and largely replaced by plastic tubing serving the same purpose.

Batten. A wooden or plastic stiffener inserted into a pocket stitched into the leach of a sail.

Beam. The extreme breadth of a vessel.

Bear away. To turn a sailing vessel away from the wind.

Beaufort Scale. The scale of wind forces commonly used in meteorological forecasts.

Becket. An eye at the end of a rope. A handle for lifting a mooring buoy out of the water.

Belay. To secure a rope round a cleat.

Bend. To fix sails on to spars ready for hoisting.

Beneaped. Description of a vessel which has gone aground on top of a tide and which remains there if the next tide is not high enough to refloat her. At the extreme the period could be as long as fourteen days where the vessel goes aground on the spring tide.

Bight. Loop or slack in a rope. Geographically a large bay, e.g. the Bight of Benin.

Bilge keels. Plate keels affixed to the bilges of small yachts. Whilst giving a satisfactory lateral resistance to the water when sailing to windward they also hold the vessel upright on taking ground.

Binnacle. Fixed casing, usually capable of interior lighting, to hold a compass.

Block. A pulley equipped with one or more sheaves which gives a mechanical purchase.

Boom. A spar to which is fitted the foot of a sail. The same term is sometimes applied to posts marking the sides of a channel.

Bosun's chair. A seat equipped with slings used in hoisting a man aloft for work on masts or rigging.

Bottle screw. A coupling turning on two threaded pins so as to draw them together. Used principally in adjusting the tension on standing rigging.

Bow. The fore end of a boat.

Bowsprit. A spar set in the bow to which foresails are secured.

Brace of shakes. Derived from the shaking of a sail in the wind; a short space of time.

Break ground. Moving an anchor out of the ground either by hauling on the chain or warp or by sailing up on to it.

Bridle. A rope made fast at both ends and controlled from the centre.

Burgee. A triangular flag, sometimes bearing the badge of a club, flown at the masthead. It indicates the apparent wind to the helmsman of a sailing vessel under way.

By and large. Sailing with the wind near the beam. Colloquially, 'broadly speaking'.

By the lee. Having the wind coming from the same side as a sailing vessel is carrying the mainsail.

By the wind. Sailing close hauled without starving the sails of wind.

C

Can buoy. Circular flat-topped buoy. Marks the port hand of a channel from the seaward if painted red or chequered red and white.

Careen. To heave a vessel on her side to expose the underwater parts.

Carry away. To break a rope, spar or fitting.

Carrying helm. A small correction by the helm necessary to check any continuous tendency for a vessel to wander off course.

Carvel-built. Planking laid edge to edge.

Cast off. Let go mooring ropes or chain.

Catspaw. Ripples on the water indicating an approaching puff of wind.

Centreboard, centreplate or daggerboard. A retractable keel used in sailing dinghies, now found increasingly in larger yachts.

Chain plate. Metal fittings fixed to the sides of a boat to which shrouds are secured.

Chart datum. A level below which low tides are unlikely to fall.

Chine. Intersections of the seams of a plywood boat or of straight sides with a flat bottom.

Class boats. Craft built to a design from which little or no deviation is allowed.

Cleat. A two-horned metal or wood fitting to which a rope may be secured.

Clevis pin. A plain metal pin, headed at one end and drilled at the other. Used to secure rigging to a horse-shoe shaped fitting, being kept in position by a safety or split pin passed through the hole drilled at the outer end.

Clew. The lower corner of the after edge of a sail.

Clinker-built. Planking laid so that it overlaps.

Cocked hat. In calculating a position on a chart three bearing lines are drawn. Seldom coinciding, a small triangle is the result and the middle of this is taken as the vessel's approximate position.

Conical buoy. Painted black or black-and-white chequered, a conical buoy marks the starboard hand of a channel when the tide is flooding.

Cross-trees. Struts fixed to the mast to spread the shrouds.

Cutting. Tides are at their highest during springs. After the highest spring tides of any series they begin to cut to neaps.

D

Daggerboard. A retractable keel not fixed to a pivot.

Dead reckoning. Position on a chart of a vessel calculated by the use of log, compass and tide tables and without the use of a sextant.

Deviation. Compass error caused by magnetic action of iron parts of a vessel. Deviations are periodically checked by swinging the ship through all points of the compass and recording differences on a deviation card.

Displacement. The actual weight of a vessel as measured by the amount of water which it displaces.

Dodger. A spray screen made of canvas or other material.

Double-ender. A vessel pointed at bow and stern.

Double-tide. Currents running from two different directions at each flood (as round the Isle of Wight into the Solent) bringing two high water times to each tide.

Downhaul (spinnaker). A bracing to hold the spinnaker boom in the correct position (see also *Topping lift*).

Down helm. Putting the helm down to leeward so as to turn a vessel up into the wind.

Drag, to. An anchor which fails to take a hold on the bottom causes a vessel to drag.

Drogue. A sea anchor made of canvas in the shape of a cone used in very deep water to keep the head of a vessel to the wind. Usually used in gale conditions.

E

Ease helm. Putting the helm down slightly when sailing to windward.

Ease sheets. Slacken off sails to lessen the way of a sailing boat.

Ebb. The falling tide.

Equinox. The two periods of the year at spring and autumn when day and night are of equal length. Unusually high tides occur at the equinoxes and are often accompanied by gales.

Eye of the wind. The direction from which the wind is blowing.

Eye splice. An end to a rope in which the strands are tucked to form a loop in which may be enclosed a thimble to form a hard eye. Without the thimble it is termed a soft eye.

F

Fair wind. Any wind which allows a sailing boat to follow a course without tacking.

Fairlead. Any fitting which acts as a guide for a rope.

Fairway. A navigable channel.

Fall away. Turning from the wind so as to make excessive leeway.

Fathom. Six feet.

Fetch. To lay a mark or other objective in one tack.

Flood. Incoming tide; high water.

Forestay. A wire stay running from the mast to the stem of the boat for support purposes.

Forward (pronounced 'forrard'). Towards the bow.

Freeboard. Height from the level of the water to the gunwale.

Full and by. Sailing as close to the wind as possible whilst keeping the sails full of wind.

G

Garboards. Planking running parallel with the keel and next to it.

Gather way. Start to move through the water so that the helm is effective.

Ghosting. Having steerage way on a sailing boat when no wind is apparent.

Gimbals. A suspension fitting made with two concentric jointed rings so as to keep a compass bowl or a cooking stove in a horizontal plane regardless of the motion of a vessel.

Gingerbread. The carved designs formerly decorating the poops or sterns of vessels. These were frequently gilded and after a rough passage the 'gilt was off the gingerbread'.

Gooseneck. A sliding fitting on the after side of the mast from which projects a spike on to which the inner end of the boom is fixed.

Grapnel. Small anchor having more than two flukes usually used for locating a mooring chain which has parted from the buoy, etc.

Ground tackle. Chains, cable and anchors used for laying out a mooring.

Gudgeon. Fitting fixed to a sternpost into which the rudder pintle is shipped.

Gunwale. Upper edge of the topsides.

H

Halyard. A rope used for hoisting a sail.

Haul the wind. To sail closer to the wind after running free.

Head board. A piece of flat wood, usually triangular in shape, sewn into the head of the mainsail.

Headway. Forward movement through the water.

Heaving down. Pulling a vessel over on her side by using tackles fixed to the masthead and the shore.

Hog. A timber running fore and aft, fixed to and above the keel.

Holding ground. Mud, sand or shingle bottom is usually good anchor holding ground: rock or pebble may be poor. For these reasons the nature of the bottom in shoal waters is marked on charts.

Holiday. A patch accidentally left uncovered by paint or varnish.

Horse. A metal bar or grooved fitting fastened athwartships so as to permit the movement of the mainsheet across the boat when it is laid from one tack to another.

Hounds. A metal fitting fixed to the mast to which forestay and shrouds are attached.

Hove to. A vessel is hove to when sails and helm are adjusted so as to offset each other, the vessel then making no way through the water.

I

In irons. Head to wind and making no way.

In stays. Going from one tack to the other over the wind.

Inboard. Towards midships: within the structure of a vessel.

Inshore. Towards the shore.

Inwale. A term still occasionally used for gunwale.

Iron topsail. Any auxiliary engine.

J

Jibstick. Spar for spreading out the foresail when running goosewinged.

Jill along. To move slowly through the water with sheets deliberately eased.

Jump the gun. Cross the starting line in a race just before the starting gun is fired.

Jury-rig. Usually applied to any method devised to spread sail after dismasting, but can mean anything temporarily fixed to substitute for broken gear.

Jury rudder. Any device to enable a boat to be steered after damage to or loss of the rudder.

K

Ketch. Two-masted sailing vessel carrying the shorter mizzen mast aft and stepped forward of the rudder-head.

Kicking-strap. A rope or wire connected to the boom and the bottom of the mast, having the function of preventing the boom from 'skying' on a gybe and generally making the mainsail more efficient in driving to windward.

Killick. A weight used for anchoring light boats.

Kite. Usually applied to lightweight spinnakers for use in light winds, but equally descriptive of any light foresail.

Knot. One nautical mile per hour.

L

Landfall. A first sighting of land after a voyage in open water. A good landfall is one which brings the vessel to the point calculated.

Lanyard. Any short piece of rope made up to perform a particular function.

Larboard. Former term for port as opposed to starboard, still occasionally used by fishermen.

Lay off a course. To calculate and mark off a course on a chart.

Lay out a kedge. Move an anchor and a warp in a tender from a larger vessel. When the anchor is dropped over the side the warp, taken aboard the parent vessel, is used to move it to a new position.

Leach. The after edge of a fore-and-aft sail.

Leading mark. Usually in pairs and brought into lines to give a direction for bringing a vessel into a haven. Leading marks are prominent features easily distinguished from the seaward.

Lee (side of a boat). The side of a boat farthest from the wind; a shelter from the wind; a lee shore is that on to which the wind is blowing.

Leeboards. Large swivelling boards functioning as drop-keels in vessels such as the Thames barge and many Dutch barge types.

Leebowing the tide. Sailing to windward and having a tide thrusting against the lee bow, so saving the boat from making leeway.

Leeward. Downwind. (Pronounced 'looard').

Leeway. The difference in angle between the line upon which a sailing vessel is heading and the line actually made good.

Let fly. Free a sheet completely so as to spill wind from the sail.

Log. Any device for measuring the speed and distance covered through the water.

Lubber line. Black line parallel with the fore-and-aft line of a vessel and marked inside the bowl of a compass.

Luff (of a sail). The leading edge of the sail. Foresails usually have a wire sewn into the luff and mainsails invariably have a rope stitched in.

M

Make fast. Secure by a rope (a dinghy to a post, bollard, etc.).

Make sail. Hoist sails.

Making. A rising tide is said to be 'making'.

Mean. Average.

Miss stays. Failure to go about through 90° when changing tack, followed by falling off on to the original tack.

Mitre. A diagonal seam running from the clew of a foresail towards the luff.

Mooring. An arrangement of anchors and chains laid on the bottom from which rises a lighter mooring chain: this lighter chain is attached to a buoy, usually by a rope strop.

N

Nautical almanac. Astronomical tables and other information for use in navigating.

Nautical mile. 6,080 ft, approximately 2,000 yards.

Neaped. A vessel which has gone aground on the top of a tide and which fails to float on the next tide is said to be 'neaped'.

O

Observed position. Actual position plotted on a chart from observations and bearings taken on fixed objects, as opposed to a dead reckoning position worked out by calculation.

Officer of the day. A club official in charge of racing arrange-
    ments for a particular day.

Offshore. At some distance from the shore.

On the wind. Sailing close-hauled.

Out of trim. Down by the bow or stern or listing unduly.

Outhaul. A lanyard arranged so as to tauten a sail on a boom or
    to pull anything out.

Outpoint. Sailing more closely to the wind than another vessel.

Overfall. Sharply breaking waves at the meeting of conflicting
    currents.

P

Patent log. An instrument for the measurement of distance run
    through the water, operated by a vane on a rotating line.

Pintle. Metal pin fixed vertically to the sternpost, on which the
    rudder is hung.

Pooped. To have a wave break over the stern in a following sea.

Port. Left-hand side of the boat looking forward.

Positive buoyancy. An important factor in small boats, enabling
    it to stay afloat when waterlogged.

Protest flag. A flag flown from a shroud during a race to signify
    that a protest will be made later in respect of another com-
    petitor, perhaps more than one. In dinghies a handkerchief
    is usually tied to a shroud.

Pulpit. Metal guardrail fitted at bow or stern of cruising yachts.

Q

Quarter. Side of the boat towards the stern.

R

Race. A strong current set up by a tide.

Rake. Inclination of a mast forward or aft of the vertical.

Reeve. Passing a rope through a fairlead or block, etc.

Roach. A curve in the leach of a sail extending outward from a
    line between the clew and the head.

Round to. Point up into wind deliberately, as when losing way
    on coming up to a mooring buoy.

Rowlock. A swivelling metal crutch to receive an oar whilst
    rowing.

S

Sag. Fall away to leeway needlessly.

Sailing committee. Sub-committee of a sailing club which arranges and controls racing fixtures.

Scandalize. Reduce the drive of a mainsail by hauling on the topping lift.

Sea breeze. A wind blowing from seaward, often locally.

Shackle. A metal fitting to connect one piece of gear with another.

Shake out a reef. Unreefing a sail either partially or wholly.

Sheave. Wheel in a block or other fitting over which a rope is rove.

Sheet(s). A rope or ropes used for controlling a sail.

Shorten sail. Reduce the sail area by reefing or lowering sails, or by substituting smaller sails.

Shrouds. Stays, usually made of wire, supporting the mast on either side of the boat.

Snubbing. Jerking at a warp or chain whilst anchored, caused by short seas. If allowed to continue the anchor may start to drag.

Spinnaker. A large foresail set on the side opposite to the mainsail when running.

Spinnaker guy. A rope running from the outer end of the spinnaker boom and passing through a special fairlead fixed to the quarter of the boat.

Spinnaker sheet. A rope fixed to the free corner of a spinnaker and passing through a special fairlead fixed to the quarter of the boat. When the spinnaker is gybed the guy and the sheet exchange their functions.

Splice. A method of joining two ropes by weaving the strands together.

Spoil ground. An area of deep water marked off in charts and into which dredgers discharge.

Spreaders. Horizontal wood or metal struts fitted to the mast to spread the shrouds.

Sprung. A spar or mast which has been strained and weakened is said to be 'sprung'.

Stand by. Be ready.

Standing rigging. Fixed rigging having the function of supporting the mast. It includes forestays, shrouds and, in some cases, a backstay leading down to the stern.

Starboard. Right-hand side of a vessel looking forward; said to derive from the fact that the steering oar or board was lowered over this side at the stern.

Stempost. A timber at the bow into which the side planking is butted.

Stern. Rear of the boat.

Sternway. Backward movement of a vessel.

Stick on the putty. Go aground on a mudbank.

Storm cone. Stations ashore, always marked on charts, hoist large black cones as gale warnings. If the cone points downward the gale is expected from the south, if upwards, from the north.

Swig. Tautening a rope by taking a half turn round a cleat with one hand and hauling with the other.

T

Tabernacle. Housing for the foot of a mast, often incorporating a pivot to ease the operation of lowering it.

Thwart. A seat placed across a boat at a right angle to the keel.

Tide rode. Riding head to tide on an anchor or mooring.

Tiller. A shaped piece of wood, usually removable, fitted into the head of the rudder to give lateral movement. To it is frequently fitted a hinged extension used when 'sitting out' the boat.

Tingle. A metal plate fastened over the holed side of a vessel.

Tonnage. Measurement of the size of a vessel: gross tonnage is calculated upon the cubic capacity below decks, Thames measurement (T.M.) upon the length of decked-in space and the maximum beam. The latter method will produce the highest figure for a given vessel.

Topping lift. Tackle for taking the weight of the main boom whilst the sail is hauled up: it is slackened off when the sail has been hoisted. Usually used only on keel boats having fairly heavy spars. Used with a spinnaker to adjust the boom to the correct position in conjunction with the downhaul: a portion of the topping lift is often made of rubber shock cord.

Transom. After portion of the hull to which rudder fittings are fitted.

Tripping the anchor. Shortening up the chain or warp so that the anchor breaks out of the ground.

Trot. A line of buoys from each of which mooring chains run down to a heavier ground chain, which is usually secured by a pair of heavy anchors at each end.

U

Undertow. A current below the surface running in a direction different to that at water level.

V

Vang. A rope passed round the boom of a vessel running down-wind to stop the spar rising and spilling wind as the craft rolls.

Veer. Let out chain or warp.

W

Warp. 1. Rope used for securing a vessel or moving it: a tow-rope.
2. Move a vessel by hauling it with ropes.

Weather. Leave an object or vessel to leeward.

Weather (side of a boat). The side nearest to the wind.

Weather shore. The windward shore, from which the wind is blowing.

Weigh the anchor. Haul in and break out the anchor from the bottom.

Whip. A twine binding round the end of a rope to prevent fraying.

Whisker pole. Another term for 'jibstick'.

Wind-rode. Riding head to wind on an anchor or mooring.

Wind shadow. An area of turbulent air to the leeward of a sailing boat which may blanket the sails of another.

Y

Yankee. A type of large masthead foresail.

Yawl. Two-masted sailing vessel carrying the shorter mizzen mast aft and stepped abaft of the rudder head.

APPENDIX B
KNOTS

FIGURE OF EIGHT

REEF

ROUND TURN AND
TWO HALF HITCHES

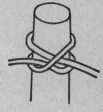

CLOVE HITCH

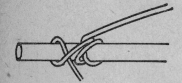

ROLLING HITCH

SHEET BEND

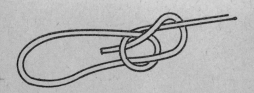

BOWLINE

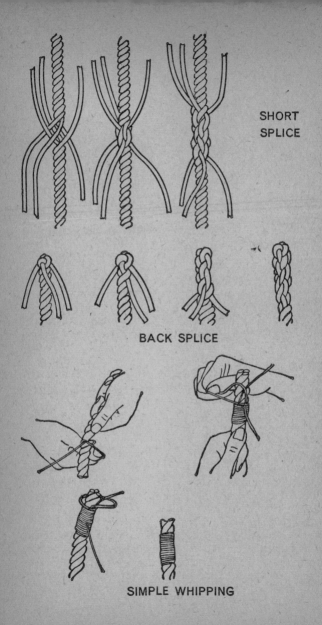

SHORT SPLICE

BACK SPLICE

SIMPLE WHIPPING

APPENDIX C

The Royal Yachting Association, 171 Victoria Street, Westminster, London, S.W.1

The national body should be supported by all who go to sea in small boats, and the different categories of membership provide the funds which enable the Association to safeguard an unspoiled coastline, champion the provision of new amenities, assist in the selecting and financing of Olympic teams and generally fight our battles.

The mounting costs of rescue services prompted the Ministry of Transport to consider the introduction of legislation to ensure that helmsmen should not take small boats to sea without any knowledge of the problems involved. Foreseeing a system of examiners, licences and tests of competency, inevitably leading to taxation, the Royal Yachting Association persuaded the Ministry that it should handle the matter.

Representatives of Sailing Schools and other teaching bodies known to the RYA elected their own representatives to a working party. Syllabi of instruction in Dinghy Sailing and in the handling of small powerboats were drawn up and approved by the Council of the RYA. Holders of Certificates of Capability qualify for considerable discounts on insurance, hire purchase rates and charter: for details you should write direct to the Federation of Sailing and Powerboat Schools, 59 Bath Road, Emsworth, Hampshire.

The Sailing Schools which have been recognized by the R.Y.A. have been inspected, the probity of principals established, and the seaworthiness of craft and safety appliances approved. Supervision and the renewal of recognition is on an annual footing and Schools not maintaining the required standards may be removed from the list.

On the next page are the Schools recognized by the RYA which are members of the Federation of Sailing and Powerboat Schools: there are others where entry is confined to certain groups, i.e. the school is associated with, for example, a particular youth hostel. Information about the Federation may be obtained from 59 Bath Road, Emsworth, Hampshire.

CORNWALL

Little Falmouth Sailing School,
Flushing,
NR. FALMOUTH.
Tel : Flushing 331.

St. Mawes Sailing School,
ST MAWES.
Tel : St Mawes 409.

Les Ferris Sailing School,
13 Polvarth Estate,
ST MAWES.

Westerly School of Sailing,
ROCK, WADEBRIDGE.
Tel : Trebetherick 3139.

Fowey River Sailing Centre,
Whitewalls, North Street,
FOWEY.
Tel : Fowey 2318.

Polruan Pool Sailing Centre,
Hillcrest, Polruan,
FOWEY.
Tel : Polruan 255.

DEVON

Newton Ferrers Sailing School Ltd.,
Westerly, Yealm Road,
NEWTON FERRERS.
Tel : Newton Ferrers 375.

Plymouth Sailing School,
34 Woolster Street, The Barbican,
PLYMOUTH.
Tel : Plymouth 67961.

Torbay Sailing School
(Brixham) Ltd.,
Breakwater Hard,
BRIXHAM.

DORSET

Poole School of Sailing,
15 Burton Road,
POOLE.
Tel : Westbourne 65194.

Seascope Sailing School,
162 Lake Road, Hamworthy,
POOLE.

ESSEX

South Eastern Sailing,
The Enterprise,
BURNHAM ON CROUCH.
Tel : Burnham on Crouch 2331.

HAMPSHIRE

Bursledon Sailing School,
The Boathouse, Old Bursledon,
NR. SOUTHAMPTON.

Coastal Courses Ltd.,
46 South Street,
EMSWORTH.
Tel : Emsworth 2914.

Emsworth Sailing School Ltd.,
Bath Road,
EMSWORTH.
Tel : Emsworth 3743.

Enterprise Sailing School,
2 Needles View, Keyhaven,
LYMINGTON.
Tel : Milford on Sea 2742.

Solent School of Yachting,
The Quay,
WARSASH.
Tel : Locksheath 3033.

ISLE OF WIGHT

Rosanna Sailing School,
Wootton Creek,
ISLE OF WIGHT.

Dodnor Creek Christian Sailing
Centre, Dodnor Creek,
NEWPORT, ISLE OF WIGHT.
Tel : Newport 2195.

MIDDLESEX

Enterprise School of Sailing,
151 Hall Road,
ISLEWORTH.
Tel : Twickenham Green 4721.

NORFOLK

Broads School of Sailing and
Seamanship,
34 Riverside, Martham,
NR. GREAT YARMOUTH.

Hunstanton Sailing School,
9b Boaton Square,
HUNSTANTON.

SCOTLAND

Loch Earn Sailing School,
Westerton House, Ochtertyre,
CRIEFF, PERTHSHIRE.
Tel : Crieff 292.

Tighnabruaich Sailing School,
TIGHNABRUAICH, ARGYLL.

SOMERSET

Southwest Small Boat School,
55 South Road,
WESTON SUPER MARE.
Tel: Weston super Mare 2857.

SUFFOLK

Pinmill Sailing Company,
Clamp House, Pinmill,
NR. IPSWICH.
Tel: Woolverstone 266.

SUSSEX

Bosham Sea School Ltd.,
The Old Malt House,
OLD BOSHAM.
Tel: Bosham 2112.

Chichester Harbour Sailing School,
Lighters Field, Tuffs Hard,
BOSHAM.

Itchenor Sailing School,
Itchenor,
NR. CHICHESTER.
Tel: Birdham 549.

Littlehampton Sailing School,
57 Harlyn Drive,
PINNER, MIDDLESEX.

Pagham Sailing Tuition,
46 Lagoon Road, Pagham Beach,
BOGNOR REGIS.
Tel: Pagham 3003.

WALES

P.G.L. Holidays Sailing Centre,
Adventure House, Station Street,
ROSS ON WYE.

Scimitar Sailing School,
Soldiers Point,
HOLYHEAD, ANGLESEY.
Tel: Tynygongl 489.

WESTMORLAND

Calgarth Hall Outdoor Pursuits
Centre,
WINDERMERE.
Tel: Windermere 2933.

SYLLABUS FOR INSTRUCTION IN POWERBOATS

Holders of Certificates must have a reasonable theoretical knowledge of the following:

(a) Nautical terms for the parts of a boat and the names and uses of individual items of that boat's equipment.

(b) Common nautical terms, e.g. Port, Starboard, Forestay, Leading mark, Buoy, Shoal, etc.

(c) The International Regulations for Preventing Collisions at Sea and the Royal Society for the Prevention of Accidents pamphlet 'Safety Afloat'.

(d) Local bye-laws affecting navigation and where to obtain such information when cruising in unfamiliar waters.

(e) The maker's instructions for running and maintaining the engine.

And have in addition attained a reasonable standard of practical competence in handling the craft in both open and restricted waters, picking up a man overboard and coming alongside.

SYLLABUS FOR INSTRUCTIONAL COURSES ON BASIC DINGHY SAILING AND ELEMENTARY SEAMANSHIP

During the course all students should wear personal buoyancy whether or not they are able to swim.

FIRST PHASE

Talk on Safety Precautions.

Introductory talk by chief instructor emphasizing that small-boat sailing, although basically a safe sport, can be dangerous unless it is approached in the right way.

Practical—Knots, i.e. reef knot, clove hitch, sheet bend, bowline and round turn and two half hitches. Rowing.

Preliminary Instruction.

Lecture by an instructor using either a real sailing dinghy or a large-scale model covering the following points:

(a) The names of the parts of the boat and their functions.
(b) Explanation of simple sea terms (e.g. Port, Starboard, Abeam, Aft) and buoyage systems.
(c) The rigging of a sailing dinghy. Characteristics of different rigs.
(d) The importance of adequate buoyancy and safety precautions for the boat and its crew.
(e) Short explanation of how a boat sails.
(f) Explanation of the difference between tidal and non-tidal sailing.

Practical demonstration by instructor of :

(a) Rigging the boat.
(b) Reefing the sails.
(c) The correct method of placing the dinghy on its launching trolley.
(d) Launching the dinghy.
(e) Boarding craft at moorings.

Preliminary instruction afloat during which the instructor demonstrates the three basic points of sailing, reaching, running, beating, and the two basic manoeuvres, tacking and gybing, and continues to demonstrate the effects of sitting out, luffing, and easing the mainsheet to spill wind. Pupils should be made to sail the boat on a reach until they have become accustomed to the feel of the tiller. When they have done this they should begin to practise sailing the boat close hauled. The instructor should stress the importance of never having the mainsheet made fast in a small boat. Pupils should then practise going about. The instructor takes the tiller again and demonstrates the importance of 'letting go all sheets' if in trouble. He explains – with practical demonstration – when to keep clear as laid down in the International Regulations for Preventing Collisions at Sea and the importance of keeping well clear of large yachts and power craft in confined waters. Pupils practise the above.

SECOND PHASE

(a) Explanation of how to right a capsized dinghy.
(b) Instructor demonstrates a gybe and pupils practise this.
(c) Instructor demonstrates the importance of tacking downwind and the risk of gybing in heavy weather.
(d) Pupils practise these manoeuvres.

THIRD PHASE

(a) Instruction in how to sail a dinghy off a lee shore after going aground and how to leave and approach the shore under varying wind conditions. He explains the meaning of on-shore and off-shore winds, and demonstrates their effect on a boat leaving and approaching a hard.

FOURTH PHASE

(a) Instruction in picking up moorings and recovering 'Man overboard'.
(b) Instructor then demonstrates these manoeuvres (preferably at slack water if sailing in water subject to strong tidal currents).

FIFTH PHASE

(a) Pupils practise all the manoeuvres learnt so far.
(b) Instruction in anchoring and in handling the dinghy whilst being towed.

GENERAL

Instruction ashore should include basic meteorology and forecasting as well as knowledge of the International Regulations for Preventing Collisions at Sea. Students should know the local bye-laws affecting yachting and how to obtain this knowledge when sailing in other waters.

INSTRUCTION HOURS NECESSARY

The minimum number of hours to cover this syllabus is considered to be:

With one student per instructor:

8 hours accompanied tuition and 4 hours when the student is in charge, excluding shore instruction.

With more than one student per instructor:

20 hours accompanied tuition and 4 hours when the student is in charge, excluding shore instruction.

APPENDIX D

INDEX OF ADDRESSES

Builders

Aln Boatyard, Alnmouth, Northumberland.

Aquacraft Ltd., Bridport, Dorset.

Auto-Marine Services Ltd., Strand Boatyard, Grove Park Road, London, W.4.

Bell Woodworking Co. Ltd., Narborough Road South, Braumstone, Leicester.

Berthon Boat Company Ltd., Lymington, Hants.

Birdham Shipyard Ltd., Birdham Pool, Chichester, Sussex.

C. S. Blanks Ltd., South Street, Stanstead Abbots, Herts.

Bossoms Boatyard Ltd., Medley, Oxford.

Camper & Nicholson Ltd., Northam, Southampton, Hants.

Cheverton & Partners Ltd., 31 Bath Road, Cowes, Isle of Wight.

Chippendale Boats Ltd., Lower Quay, Fareham, Hants.

Dell Quay Yacht Ltd., Dell Quay, Chichester, Sussex, *and* Little Quay, Old Bosham, Chichester, Sussex.

Esa Marine, The Boathouse, Digbeth, Birmingham, 5.

Fairey Marine Ltd., Hamble, Southampton, Hants, *and* Ray Mead Boathouse, Maidenhead, Berks.

Fenn and Wood Ltd., Mill Lane, Taplow, Bucks.

Freezer & Co. Ltd., Mill Rithe, Hayling Island, Hants.

Gmach & Co. Ltd., Fordingbridge, Hants.

Halmatic Ltd., Industrial Estate, Havant, Hants.

Harrison, J. H., 19 Scott Street, Largs, Ayrshire.

Holt Ltd., Jack, The Embankment, Putney, London, S.W.15.

Honnor Marine Ltd., Seymour Wharf, Totnes, Devon.

Hurley Ltd., A. G., Richmond Walk, Plymouth, Devon.

Mariners Shipyard Ltd., Old Bosham, Chichester, Sussex.

Melville Marine (Perth) Ltd., Lower Harbour, Perth, Scotland.

Moody & Son Ltd., A. H., Swanwick Shore, Southampton, Hants.

Moore & Sons Ltd., R., Station Road, Wroxham, Norfolk.

Norvalls (Smallcraft) Ltd., Royston Works, Royston Avenue, Prittlewell, Southend-on-Sea, Essex.

Parham & Sons, J. G., Queen Street, Emsworth, Hants.

Pimms Marine Ltd., Chertsey Street, Guildford, Surrey.

Plycraft Ltd., Clevedon, Somerset.

Prout & Sons Ltd., G., The Point, Canvey Island, Essex.

Sail Craft Ltd, Waterside, Brightlingsea, Essex.

Sandwich Boatyard, Sandwich, Kent.

Scutt Ltd., Gordon, Remenham Hill, Henley-on-Thames, Oxon.

Souter, W. A., 148 Arctic Road, Cowes, Isle of Wight.

South Devon Boatbuilders, 2 Iddesleigh Terrace, Dawlish, Devon.

Sprite Boats Ltd., Fordham Road, Newmarket, Cambs.

Tough Bros. Ltd., Teddington Wharf, Teddington, Middx.

Wilgate Ltd., 190 Coulsdon Road, Caterham, Surrey.

Wych & Coppock Ltd., Radford Hill, Norten Street, Nottingham.

Woodnutt & Co. Ltd., Stone Pier, Warsash, Southampton, Hants.

Wyvern Boats Ltd., Milbourne Port, Sherborne, Dorset.

Yardley & Co. Ltd., William, Burnham-on-Crouch, Essex.

Yealm Boat Co., Bridgend, Newton Ferrers, Devon.

Chandlers

Beale Ltd., Arthur, 194 Shaftesbury Avenue, London, W.C.2.

Best & Boulton Ltd., The Boathouse, 66 Princess Avenue, Hull, Yorks.

Birmingham Yacht Centre, 43 Brighton Road, Birmingham, 12.

Boat Centre Co. Ltd., 146 London Road, Leicester.

Boat Showrooms of London Ltd., 288 Kensington High Street, London, W.14.

Bosun's Locker, 65 East Street, Chichester, Sussex.

Brighton Boating Centre, 17 Upper St. James's Street, Brighton, Sussex.

Burnham Yachting Stores Ltd., The Quay, Burnham-on-Crouch, Essex.

E.S.A. Ltd., 166 Shaftesbury Avenue, London, W.C.2.

Falmouth Chandlers Ltd., High Street, Falmouth, Cornwall.

Foredeck, The, 82 High Street, Cowes, Isle of Wight.

Foulkes, Thomas, Lansdowne Road, Leytonstone, London, E.11.

Harper Marine Ltd., 359 High Street, Rochester, Kent.

London Yacht Centre Ltd., 9 Devonshire Row, London, E.C.2.

North Wales Boat Shop, The Bridge, Glan Conway.

Offshore (Sailing) Ltd., Salcombe, Devon, *and* West Street, Chichester, Sussex.

Rekab Marine, 263 High Holborn, London, W.C.1.

Thames Marine Store (J. G. Meakes), Marlow, Bucks.

Watts Ltd., Captain O. M., 49 Albemarle Street, London, W.1.

Charter and Hire

Allen & Son Ltd., Ash Island Slipway, East Molesey, Surrey.

Blackwater Yacht Charters Ltd., 31 London Road, Maldon, Essex.

Blakes (Norfolk Broads Holidays) Ltd., 47 Albemarle Street, London, W.1.

Blue Waters Charters, Soundings, Raleigh Road, Salcombe, Devon.

Bossoms Boatyard Ltd., Medley, Oxford.

Channel Yacht Charters Ltd., Rosetree House, Boxgrove, Chichester, Sussex.

Crouch Yacht Charters, Sea End Boathouse, Burnham-on-Crouch, Essex.

Dell Quay Yacht Yard Ltd., Little Quay, Old Bosham, Chichester, Sussex.

Dolphin Quay, Queen Street, Emsworth, Hants.

Falmouth Boat Construction Ltd., High Street, Falmouth, Cornwall.

Lymington Light Craft Ltd., North Close, Lymington, Hants.

Martham Boats, Martham, Great Yarmouth, Norfolk.

Moore & Sons, Wroxham, Norfolk.

Poole Harbour Charters, Panorama Road, Sandbanks, Bournemouth, Hants.

Salcombe Yacht Agency Ltd., Salcombe, Devon.

Shannon Craft Hire Ltd., 81 Grafton Street, Dublin, Eire.

Solent Services Ltd., The Quay, Warsash, Southampton, Hants.

South Coast Yacht Charters, 43 Birmingham Road, Cowes, Isle of Wight

Windermere Lake Holidays Afloat Ltd., Bowness-on-Windermere, Cumberland.

World Holidays Afloat Ltd., 9 High Road, East Finchley, London, N.2.

Clothing and Personal Buoyancy

Beale Ltd., Arthur, 194 Shaftesbury Avenue, London, W.C.2.

Boat Showrooms of London Ltd., 288 Kensington High Street, London, W.14.

Bosun's Locker, 65 East Street, Chichester, Sussex.

Bowker & Budd Ltd., Old Bosham, Chichester, Sussex.

Burnham Yachting Stores Ltd., The Quay, Burnham-on-Crouch, Essex.

Crewsaver Dinghy Equipment Ltd., North Cross Street, Gosport, Hants.

E.S.A. Marine Ltd., 166 Shaftesbury Avenue, London, W.C.2.

Foredeck, The, 82 High Street, Cowes, Isle of Wight.

Foulkes, Thomas, Lansdowne Road, Leytonstone, London, E.11.

Gardiner & Co., 1 Commercial Road, London, E.1.

Gordon Lowe Sports, Brompton Arcade, Knightsbridge, London, S.W.1.

Great Grimsby Coal, Salt & Tanning Co. Ltd., Fish Dock Road, Grimsby, Lincs.

Hall Ltd., Harry, 235 Regent Street, London, W.1.

Imray & Wilson Ltd., 141 Cannon Street, London, E.C.4.

Lillywhites Ltd., Piccadilly Circus, London, W.1, *and* Sloane Street, London, S.W.1.

London Yacht Centre Ltd., 9 Devonshire Road, London, E.C.2.

Offshore (Sailing) Ltd., Salcombe, Devon, *and* West Street, Chichester, Sussex.

Rekab Marine, 263 High Holborn, London, W.C.1.

Sea Chest, 9 Quay Hill, Lymington, Hants.

Sou'marine of Brighton, 166 Kings Road Arches, Brighton, Sussex.

Watts Ltd., Capt. O. M., 49 Albemarle Street, London, W.1.

Masts and Rigging

Bowker & Budd Ltd., Old Bosham, Chichester, Sussex.

Classcraft Ltd., Eastlands Boat House, Kingston, Surrey (Steel masts).

Cranfield & Carter Ltd., River Side, Burnham-on-Crouch, Essex.

Dell Quay Yacht Yard Ltd., Pound Farm, Westhampnett Road, Chichester, Sussex (Light alloy masts).

Gillingham, W., 1 Mill Street, Poole, Dorset.

Gowen & Co. Ltd., Coast Road, West Mersea, Essex.

Hamble Sailmakers, Hamble, Hants.

Harper Marine Ltd., 359 High Street, Rochester, Kent.

Proctor Metal Masts Ltd., Ian, Brook Avenue, Warsash, Southampton, Hants.

Sales Developments Ltd., 312 High Road, South Benfleet,
Essex. (Light alloy masts.)

Sailmakers

Banks Sails, Bruce, 372 Brook Lane, Sarisbury, Southampton,
Hants.

Bowker & Budd Ltd., Old Bosham, Chichester, Sussex.

Cranfield & Carter Ltd., River Side, Burnham-on-Crouch,
Essex.

Gowen & Co. Ltd., Coast Road, West Mersea, Essex.

Hamble Sailmakers, Hamble, Hants.

Harper Marine Ltd., 359 High Street, Rochester, Kent.

Holt, Ltd., Jack, The Embankment, Putney, London, S.W.15.

Jeckells & Son Ltd., Wroxham, Norfolk.

Lucas & Son, 42 Broad Street, Old Portsmouth, Hants.

Ratsey & Lapthorn Ltd., Medina Road, Cowes, Isle of Wight.

Seahorse Sails, Brett Sail Loft, Hadleigh, Suffolk.

Tope & Co. Ltd., 12 Southside Street, Plymouth, Devon.

Windward Sails, 210 London Road, Southend-on-Sea, Essex.

War books in Pan

NON-FICTION

FICTION

You'll be
'A SILLY OLD MOO'
if you don't rush to read
THIS SAUCY, CONTROVERSIAL BOOK
based on the TV Show
THAT SHOCKED THE NATION

ALF GARNETT
ELSE 'MA' GARNETT
'MINI' RITA
'SHIRLEY TEMPLE' MIKE

Meet them all again in
JOHNNY SPEIGHT'S

TILL DEATH US DO PART

Arranged by John Burke

Now at your bookshop, price 3/6

TILL DEATH US DO PART

Not So Much a Comedy, More a Battlefield

'The Cockneys fire their big guns in all
directions . . . and the shrapnel keeps falling
on all kinds of public figures.'
NEWS OF THE WORLD

'The rampaging, howling embodiment
of all the most vulgar and odious prejudices
that slop about in the bilges
of the national mind.'
FINANCIAL TIMES

By the author of
THE SPY WHO CAME IN FROM THE COLD

The Looking-Glass War 5/-

JOHN LE CARRE

'A book of great and rare power'
FINANCIAL TIMES

'The thinking man's thriller'
NEW YORK POST

'. . . this is a devastating and tragic
record of human, not glamour, spies'
NEW YORK HERALD TRIBUNE

For information about current and
forthcoming PAN titles write to:

PAN LIST
PAN BOOKS LTD 33 TOTHILL STREET
LONDON SW1